ECONOMIC ISSUES, PROBLEMS AND PERSPECTIVES

NEOLIBERALISM

PERSPECTIVES, HISTORY AND CRITICISMS

ECONOMIC ISSUES, PROBLEMS AND PERSPECTIVES

Additional books and e-books in this series can be found on Nova's website under the Series tab.

ECONOMIC ISSUES, PROBLEMS AND PERSPECTIVES

NEOLIBERALISM

PERSPECTIVES, HISTORY AND CRITICISMS

TRAVIS GRAHAM
EDITOR

Copyright © 2019 by Nova Science Publishers, Inc.

All rights reserved. No part of this book may be reproduced, stored in a retrieval system or transmitted in any form or by any means: electronic, electrostatic, magnetic, tape, mechanical photocopying, recording or otherwise without the written permission of the Publisher.

We have partnered with Copyright Clearance Center to make it easy for you to obtain permissions to reuse content from this publication. Simply navigate to this publication's page on Nova's website and locate the "Get Permission" button below the title description. This button is linked directly to the title's permission page on copyright.com. Alternatively, you can visit copyright.com and search by title, ISBN, or ISSN.

For further questions about using the service on copyright.com, please contact:
Copyright Clearance Center
Phone: +1-(978) 750-8400   Fax: +1-(978) 750-4470   E-mail: info@copyright.com

NOTICE TO THE READER

The Publisher has taken reasonable care in the preparation of this book, but makes no expressed or implied warranty of any kind and assumes no responsibility for any errors or omissions. No liability is assumed for incidental or consequential damages in connection with or arising out of information contained in this book. The Publisher shall not be liable for any special, consequential, or exemplary damages resulting, in whole or in part, from the readers' use of, or reliance upon, this material. Any parts of this book based on government reports are so indicated and copyright is claimed for those parts to the extent applicable to compilations of such works.

Independent verification should be sought for any data, advice or recommendations contained in this book. In addition, no responsibility is assumed by the Publisher for any injury and/or damage to persons or property arising from any methods, products, instructions, ideas or otherwise contained in this publication.

This publication is designed to provide accurate and authoritative information with regard to the subject matter covered herein. It is sold with the clear understanding that the Publisher is not engaged in rendering legal or any other professional services. If legal or any other expert assistance is required, the services of a competent person should be sought. FROM A DECLARATION OF PARTICIPANTS JOINTLY ADOPTED BY A COMMITTEE OF THE AMERICAN BAR ASSOCIATION AND A COMMITTEE OF PUBLISHERS.

Additional color graphics may be available in the e-book version of this book.

Library of Congress Cataloging-in-Publication Data

ISBN: 978-1-53616-014-7

Published by Nova Science Publishers, Inc. † New York

Contents

Preface		vii
Chapter 1	Neo-Liberalism: Managing the Tension between Freedom and Equality *Algis Mickunas*	1
Chapter 2	The Neoliberal Agenda in Higher Educational Institutions: Perspectives, Impacts and the Way Forward *Gifty Oforiwaa Gyamera*	33
Chapter 3	Autocracy vs. Neoliberalism: A Ukrainian Test Case *Žilvinas Svigaris*	69
Index		101
Related Nova Publications		107

PREFACE

There are various ways to understand neo-liberalism, including through the economy, politics, education, and globalization. In Neoliberalism: Perspectives, History and Criticisms, these topics will play a role in articulating the much-debated issue of the widening gaps between the rich and the poor, the left and the right, democracy and autocracy, and the educated and left behind.

The subsequent study uses data on neoliberal discourses and practices in higher educational institutions in Ghana in order to situate neoliberalism in a historical framework, as well as examine its perception in universities.

The closing chapter explores the possibility of transitioning from isolated monoliths of oligopolies into an ecosystem of a modular economy that is based on small or medium, competitive, community friendly and flexible enterprises.

Chapter 1 - Neo-Liberalism has been praised and demonized, but its essential tasks left out of focus. The taks is basic: how to balance the two major premises of modern, political society and economy: freedom and equality. The balancing includes the relationship between the public and the private spheres in a way that both intersect and change one another. At the same time, such intersections are global and must pay attention to various social systems, containing notable differences: some are autocratic, others are liberal, still others are theocratic, each with its own rules of commerce and public/private relationships. Given this context, Neo-Liberal logic, disclosed in this essay, offers a complex and dynamic understanding of the ways that temporal possibilities and horizons – both political and commercial – intersect and offer options for the shifting relationships between freedom and equality, including it's attendant educational requirements. The latter also take into account global requirements promoted by Neo-Liberalism.

Chapter 2 - For the past few decades, neoliberalism has become a dominant ideology influencing governmental and institutional policies and practices across the world. It has transcended the political, economic, cultural and social contexts. Ghana, as a country, has not been insulated from the tentacles and influences of neoliberalism. Recently, neoliberalism has been firmly implanted and has permeating various institutions including higher education. This emphasis on neoliberalism is derived from the capitalist ideology the country was forced to adopt in the 80's due to harsh economic conditions. This study draws on data on neoliberal discourses and practices in universities in Ghana. It situates neoliberalism in a historical framework and looks at how it is perceived and manifested in various aspects of the universities, the impact and the way forward. Initial findings of the study suggest that many of the reforms which have occurred in the universities, particularly over the past two decades, were mainly informed by neoliberal ideologies. These reforms influenced varied aspects of the universities including infrastructural development, curriculum changes, expectations and demands of academics and administrators and restructuring of departments. The values, structures and processes of the private sector have been adopted by the universities. A vital element is an emphasis on 'performance' measured by quantitative outcomes. The mandates of the universities appear to have changed from knowledge creation and dissemination to production of marketable skills and promoting of entrepreneurship. All the universities are engaged in enterprising activities, competition and promoting their brand. Whilst there are some positive implications including improved infrastructural development, the disadvantages appear overwhelming. Both academics and administrators are confronted with many challenges including individualism, job insecurity and excessive stress. Inequalities and meritocracy have become the norm. In spite of these challenges, little is being done to resist the neoliberal ideologies. Both academics, administrators and senior management have accepted its performativity expectations. Everyone strives to fulfill them. The author argues for the need of academia to resist neoliberal ideologies as the dominant ideology governing universities. There should be much research into the impact of neoliberalism on higher educational institutions.

Chapter 3 - One more country decided to take a risk and see what it means to become liberal and democratic. Although liberal democracy is often considered as the best form of human government, currently it is facing a so-called neoliberal crisis that has brought unexpected and disruptive results of uneven sharing of power and wealth in society. Capital concentration in natural oligopolies and corporate control become almost unresolvable problems facing modern economies. This paper will explore here the possibilities of transitioning from isolated monoliths of oligopolies into an ecosystem of a modular economy that is based on small or medium, competitive, community friendly and flexible enterprises. This trend stimulates the creation of a self-driven society that does not depend exclusively on the local economic situation anymore but can benefit from globally accessible opportunities. Ukraine is right at the core of the geostrategic concerns and not only because of the geopolitical location of the country but mainly because it raises questions that are relevant to all liberal democracies in the world that are troubled by after-effects of neoliberal policies. Although there is still a high risk that Ukraine might end up going off the rails into the systemic corruption again, there is also hope of seeing the transformation of the current neoliberal system into a new self-driven society able to solve problems of safety and employment in the country. However, let us start with events that took place in Ukraine almost four years ago, from the Revolution of Dignity.

In: Neoliberalism
Editor: Travis Graham

ISBN: 978-1-53616-014-7
© 2019 Nova Science Publishers, Inc.

Chapter 1

NEO-LIBERALISM: MANAGING THE TENSION BETWEEN FREEDOM AND EQUALITY

Algis Mickunas
Professor Emeritus, Ohio University, Athens, OH, US

ABSTRACT

Neo-Liberalism has been praised and demonized, but its essential tasks left out of focus. The taks is basic: how to balance the two major premises of modern, political society and economy: freedom and equality. The balancing includes the relationship between the public and the private spheres in a way that both intersect and change one another. At the same time, such intersections are global and must pay attention to various social systems, containing notable differences: some are autocratic, others are liberal, still others are theocratic, each with its own rules of commerce and public/private relationships. Given this context, Neo-Liberal logic, disclosed in this essay, offers a complex and dynamic understanding of the ways that temporal possibilities and horizons – both political and commercial – intersect and offer options for the shifting relationships between freedom and equality, including it's attendant educational requirements. The latter also take into account global requirements promoted by Neo-Liberalism.

Keywords: freedom, equality, public, private, globalization, possibility, horizon, time reflection

INTRODUCTION

There are various ways to understand Neo-liberalism, extending from economy, through politics, education, all the way to globalization. In this essay, these topics will play a role as ways of articulating the much-debated issue of the widening gaps between the rich and the poor, the left and the right, democracy and autocracy, educated and left behind, and all premised on the final division between equality and freedom. It is the case that the modern West has emerged as a dominant global presence in many domains, but it also had an assumption of the conjunction between freedom and equality, specifically in the political-public domain. Each individual has an equal claim to participate in governance; this claim guarantees that in the public arena no social differences, such as wealth, family heritage, religious position, or occupation, are to be counted. The trend under consideration stems from equality with an added freedom of each individual, irrespective of social descent, to "make his own way," to shape his own destiny, owing nothing to anyone, having no masters, and placing himself in a position of being a master of himself and his survey. Some become examples of having made their own way, and indeed "on their own," irrespective of odds and oppositions. This is to say they have shown that man can make and live his life independently of others, can withdraw into "his own business," and leave the business of others to their own devices.

In this sense, the citizens, in the public domain are fully free because they are equal, such that in principle, freedom and equality are convertible. At the outset, the basis of modern freedom is equality, although subsequently freedom assumes a more fundamental role, and indeed becomes the basis for equality. One could claim that the democratic revolution is an effort to maintain the identity between the two, so that every deviation from it would be judged as anti-democratic. Yet the balance between them appears in various social compositions differently, and this provides us with a clue as to their distinguishability and the meaning of initial "liberalism" followed by neo-liberalism. There can be liberal equality in a social sphere, but not in the political; i.e., each is socially free to pursue his/her own interests but does not have political freedom with respect to the establishment of laws and participation in public decisions. There is political inequality within social equality and conversely. Indeed, there can be a total political equality and yet a complete lack of political freedom, whether under one ruler or under a collective. Their identity seems to intimate that a complete equality is identifiable with freedom, and yet, even in a democratic society, they can assume extreme opposition. Of course, the democratic revolution assumes their identity, being fully cognizant of the danger that a complete disappearance of freedom might be compatible with equality. One could point out that the more recent social dictatorships were and are compatible with equality, but with a full exclusion of freedom – as was the case with the Soviet Union. The latter example can be extended to contemporary Russia, China, various theocracies, containing diverse relationships between freedom and equality.

PUBLIC AND PRIVATE

While in the public domain all are equal and free, there is a publically-established rule that in the private domain each is equally free to pursue his personal interests, above all those of material well being. What is the impetus for this general concern? Why does it appear so prominently in the age of equality and political freedom? To grasp the significance of this state of affairs, we must consider the background from which democratic equality and freedom emerged: feudalism. In feudalism, there were two major social positions, the aristocrat and the peasant. The aristocrat possessed wealth by birthright; material wellbeing was not an object of concern – it was deemed natural. There was no need to strive for possession and its security, since there was no fear of loss of one's natural birthright. The peasant, on the other hand, was materially poor and, because of his origins, could not hope to be rich or to acquire material wealth. In this sense, material wealth could not be an object of desire for which one could strive. In principle, there is a social-private arrangement that does not allow for a political domain where everyone is free and equal. In fact, there is no need to make a distinction between private and public, since the aristocratic class was both a ruler of the public issues and all private possessions – including an ownership of the serfs. The change in this context can occur only when both classes are exposed to the possibilities of loss and gain; i.e., when the aristocrats are exposed to the loss of their possessions, and the lower class is exposed to the possibility of acquiring wealth and equal status with all members of society. Once the privileges are discarded by the decree of equality, once possibilities in every domain become open for everyone, the limits of what can be reached and attained no longer lie in one's social position, but in one's own wishes, talents, dedication, and in becoming one's own standard creator and bearer. But, this is subtended by one condition: not being bound by any birthright and privilege, the individual is no longer dependent upon, and in turn can neither depend on, nor ask for assistance from anyone; he is on his own to make his own way, shape his own destiny.

Obviously, this background comprises two factors: first, the human is in principle self-determined, autonomous, a free being, and second, in this self-determination he must determine the world by remaking it to serve his purposes. At this juncture, it should be pointed out that one of the "motives" to master nature is inherent in the democratic revolution. The authors who established political enlightenment and its inherent liberalism also set up the institutional conditions for the adjudication of what is public and what is private, resulting in the basic conception of "political economy." Thus, political decisions devised the rights of every individual to pursue his private interests freely and equally with others, forming various associations and ventures for his own advantage. The latter leads to competition resulting in winners and losers, and thus social inequality – fully cognizant that in the public domain they are still free and equal. An individual must live in an incessant striving to secure his own livelihood in competition with others and in face of a possible loss. Under these conditions, the entire social fabric becomes an arena of private striving for wellbeing, a struggle of everyone against everyone. Even the rich cannot escape this striving; having won their wealth through struggle, they have established a mode of life in which the acquisition of more and more is second nature. Indeed, the calculated striving to obtain more and more has become interpreted as a religious, moral duty, a god's way, a sign of divine favor. In this context, material inequality becomes preeminent, leading to the gap between the poor and the rich – a gap that is being constantly reported in contemporary discussions in all corners of the globe. We need not go into the protracted arguments who owns what based on the labor theory of value; our concern is the social, material domain in which the great gap appears, where one is free and equal, but at the same time one's concrete equality is gone – even if one is free not to work for someone else for survival.

The main problem that emerged for the political institutions established by enlightenment is the industrial revolution, where a large segment of the population – released from feudal conditions – had only one "property:" labor power. This is an entirely new conception of what is one's own property. It is postulated that nature in itself has no value; value comes from human activity, which gives nature its value, and such an activity is labor, grounding a theory that the primary property a person possesses is his body, the activity of which can be sold. This conception allows a subordination of one person by another in the area of social powers, creating a situation in which one group is much weaker than another group. While the modern enlightenment might want to equalize matters through laws and regulations, by themselves the latter are insufficient to achieve equality and independence. We have reached, here, a multi-faceted tension. First, there is the tension between freedom and equality – even if they are initially and in principle mutually founding. This tension becomes apparent in the democratic society where the public domain sanctions freedom and equality as inseparable, but in the social-private arena, there appear noted material inequities. Second, there is a tension between an effort to establish human mastery over nature and over traditional views of human essence. Third, there emerges a tension between the human as a source of power and mastery, and the human who becomes subject to the very power means created by the human. Fourth, the tension between the social-private demands to secure material means of wellbeing, and the requirements of maintaining the democratic public domain as a guarantee of autonomy and equality. All in all, these tensions are not a given; they depend on the requisite activities that constitute them as given.

The form of inequality is mainly addressed in terms of "rich/poor" dichotomy. We are faced with the concerns for the poor as completely unequal to the "rich and powerful," leading to a major debate among economic theorists and even at times philosophers. The issue centers on how to reduce poverty without harming economy. In order to survive, the economy has to grow instead of remaining at the level of satisfying basic needs. In the West, already from the 16th century on, the poor were seen as a necessity for a healthy economy. Educated persons such as B. de Mandeville, an economist, bluntly stated that without direct slavery the economic wealth of a nation depends directly on a vast number of working poor. Of course, this also implied that for the good of economic development, there is no need to diminish poverty. Whatever measures were offered, they were not intended to relieve poverty, but to help the poor in catastrophic cases. There were even voices claiming that the poor are at fault because of their laziness, perhaps even ungodliness and lustful life. A preacher, T. Malthus, was one of the major propagators of this view; for him economic progress depended on technology that might even help the poor, but due to the lust, the poor will produce excess offspring and thus will always be poor. His views prompted new laws that outlawed any relief and thus forced the poor to rely solely on their workplace. A. Smith proposed a vague solution in relationship to the taxes that the rich pay, but no consequences flowed from his "vision." Marx of course had his solution: abolition of private ownership of the means of production, allowing the "masses" to take control of such means and thus become owners/workers. Lenin attempted to implement Marx's views but all that was achieved was a life above the poverty line for the majority, and a luxurious life for the self-appointed "revolutionary elite," the de facto owners of all property "in the name of the people," constituting what since Djilas' time is known as "state capitalism." The Soviet "experiment" was a total failure and had to collapse due to equality without freedom.

In the 20th century, there appeared all sorts of calculations: since the rich saved more than the poor, the reduction in poverty would reduce economic growth, to which J. M. Keynes objected by pointing out that what is important for economic growth is consumption and reducing poverty would increase consumption. Following this conception, there was an explosion of evidence that any increase in poverty was correlated to decrease in investments and innovation. Computer technology opened capacities to build economic models that consistently demonstrated that unequal ability to obtain credit leads to the inability by the poor to invest in education or even small business, resulting in a diminished growth for the total economy. Of course, these views, coupled with the great depression, destroyed the myth that poor people are poor because they are lazy, alcoholic, and even stupid. The newer models also showed administrators in charge of public policy that a lack of education, health care, and proper nutrition kept people in poverty; hence, funding education, health care, and nutrition for children were not only the right thing to do, but also good for the economy and, finally, enhancing equality and freedom of choices. This is not to say that the question of the ideological divide between rich and poor is settled. To the contrary, current American conservatives in the government want not only to dismantle the "socialist" safety nets such as Medicare, Medicaid and Social Security, but use the same justifications advanced in the 19th century. Thus, senators Chuck Grassley of Iowa and Orrin Hatch of Utah argue the former claiming that rich people invest their money as opposed to those who are just spending every penny they have whether on booze, or movies, or women, and the latter stating that it makes sense to cut corporate taxes, but makes sense to reduce Obamacare and other safety-net spending since the government currently spends trillions to help people who won't help themselves, won't lift a finger. Add to this P. Ryan and the evangelicals who are apt to quote Matthew whereby it is said that "for unto everyone that hath shall be given, and he shall have abundance; but from him that hath not shall be taken even that which he hath" (Matthew 25:29). If we are in a neo-liberal age, do such proclamations represent neo-liberalism?

LIBERAL CONTEXT

Liberal, secular democracy and its various policies, accepted the principles of enlightenment. After World War II, the West (with participation and consent of over 50 nations and the U.N. (except for the Soviet Union), reached an agreement allowing for an open world of trade, of development even of small nations without military interferences, and a punishment (at least economic) of aggressors. No territorial gains would be recognized and resisted by U.N. forces. Even colonial Western states had to surrender their colonies, leading to more or less legitimate states (legitimate in the sense that the final source of legitimation of juridical or political society is the public). Not only national rule of law, but international commitment to agreements, encouraging the movement of ideas, education, cultural exchange, and voices for every nation at the United Nations, became the norm. This was the post-World War II, liberal world, championed by the United States and the recovering Europe, leading to European Union, and even promoted by Japan. (Oona Hathaway and Scott Shapiro, 2018) As noted, this liberalism was founded on the principles of freedom and equality established by modern Western Enlightenment.

In principle, it was the United States after World War II that promoted and established world-wide liberal institutions, giving each nation a stake in keeping the world peaceful and stable. It is not by accident that the World Bank, International Monetary Fund, and United Nations ended up in the U.S. For seventy years, the world was oriented toward the U.S. as a standard protector of freedom and equality, forming trade agreements, resulting in a global exchange of commodities, people, culture, and education. The world expected and accepted that United States would continue to promote and defend human rights, progress in all areas, including world health and challenging authoritarian regimes everywhere. The mentioned "political economy" was in full swing: the public domain of freedom and equality intervened in the private, economic affairs, establishing rules of safety, wages, social security, and workers' rights. Here the public and the private domains began to intersect and mix, requiring public adjudication of complex private enterprises and diverse social groups: teachers, women, students, trade workers, doctors, etc.. Liberal economy became part of it, inspired by Keynesian proposals which included the concept that the dimnishing gap between rich and poor is a benefit to economy and equality, including a freedom of opportunity.

For liberalism, the relationship between freedom and equality is complex. If equality becomes the principle of social formation, it becomes very difficult to overcome such a principle. It becomes embedded in human habits, customs, and beliefs that, under any ontological interpretation, fundamentally we are equal. Freedom remains only as long as it is insisted upon and maintained. The maintenance of equality requires no effort, while its abolition would be more difficult. Freedom requires continuous vigilance, and it vanishes by a simple neglect. The advantages of equality are obvious: all professions, all positions, aims, are open to everyone; each can attain every wish in accord with his dedication and talent. Every person has equal social conditions and advantages. The advantages of freedom are more difficult to recount. They become visible only with the disadvantages after freedom has been lost. If we strive to maintain the public sphere and free existence, our requirements change: instead of following our own individual interests, we must not only "transcend" ourselves, but be willing to maintain this transcendence in the face of our own social disadvantage. In this sense, freedom is not necessarily identical with one's social and material wishes, and its maintenance is an effort and in many cases a sacrifice. History testifies that only few were willing to rise to the level of public and demand a political society in which the socially disadvantaged were deemed politically equal to the socially advantaged, and in which the few were willing to disregard their own private concerns. Thus, once again it is obvious that the advantages of equality are easily acceptable to most, while the advantages of freedom tend to be disregarded and left out, specifically when the domain of freedom is difficult to maintain and might have no advantages in the area of social and private concerns.

If there are drawbacks in liberal democracy, there is one basic means of checking them: political freedom. The formula is shown in political logic. If freedom, which owes its realization to equality, is not to disappear behind equality, then these two determinations shaping democratic consciousness must be reversed. The democratic consciousness has assumed equality to be preeminent. In this sense, freedom can be used for the establishment of equality. But if this is not to lead to the despotism of equality, freedom must be backed by equality of freedom. This is not a surrender of equality, but rather a recognition of the main factor that made equality possible. This reversal allows the establishment of the initial equation of freedom and equality: the will to equality becomes the basis for the will to freedom, while freedom becomes the determining viewpoint for the will to equality. This is to say, the political-public domain of freedom tends to impose rules to promote equality and thus to intersect the private domain, resulting in the mixture of politics and material well-being. The fundamental phrase of this conjunction for liberalism was and still is the demand by the public and the promise by political candidates: *create jobs.*

At any rate, the legitimation of the production of increased material well-being – more things, more benefits, more enjoyment, more health, more... more, becomes self-legitimating in the face of the public's demand for more securities in the material sphere. But this raises an immediate question concerning the legitimation of the public domain. The free discourse for the public benefit is not an issue; the issue is material well-being – private. Hence, the public domain, in order to be legitimate, must be reduced to the management and accommodation of private material interests. The political parties must shift their operations toward the fulfillment of material wants. But once this shift is made, there is no turning back, since in order to be legitimate, the political parties must fulfill the material promises. Failing this, they cease to be regarded as legitimate. This is what constitutes the legitimation crisis of the political domain in modern liberalism. In order for the political parties to maintain themselves in power, they must possess material power capable of satisfying the demands of the masses – demands for greater equality – and mainly in the economic domain. The population, in turn, takes the economization for granted and exerts pressure on the systems to "produce" visible results. Failing such results, one can argue that the system has no legitimation. During free elections, the rhethoric circles on well-paying jobs, benefits, health, and security, involving, for their "production," a vast state machinery. Here, the voter regards herself as autonomous and equal. The main economic system with liberalism is the traditional notion of jobs and security: the employee is loyal to the company and the company "appreciates" and rewards such loyalty with longevity; education is identical with getting training for a "good job" and remaining in the "field" and one organization. Scholars call this model "Ford System," containing an assembly line of temporal sequence. The latter is also used as a model to explain events in economic terms: given economic conditions, we can predict future results (Bob Jessop, 2006). Under the assumption that the citizens live in a democratic society, there is no need to be concerned with public affairs – apart from an occasional time out to vote.

THE THREAT

The attacks on freedom and equality, as a basis of enightenment and liberalism, have appeared in various guises, including writings by "philosophers" of post-modern and critical ilk. They are tripping over themselves to shout that "The Project of Enlightenment" is dead (Horkheimer M. and Adorno T. 2002). Similar, "critical" pronouncements made a protracted splash with the writings of such notables as Deleuze and Guattari (2009). More bad news appear in most recent writings with pronouncements of a complete failure of liberalism, as is depicted above. Patrick Deneen (2018) claims that the founding tenents of liberalism's faith have been shattered. Equality of opportunity has produced a new meritocratic aristocracy with none of its commitment to public responsibility. Indeed, the widening gap of inequality is global and the solution to such inequality is also facing a gap between rigidified ideologies of left and right to such an extent that there is no discourse between them. In short, the gap between liberalism's claims of freedom and equality is so different from reality, that no lies can fill such a gap. To understand the extent of the collapse, more recent global phenomena must be introduced.

The emergence of nationalisms, closed upon themselves, with autocratic tendencies and extoling their efficiency as better suited to benefit the populations, must replace Western liberalism, which has become morally corrupt and "soft," is gaining popularity. Rational thinking, philosophy as the "erotic aim for wisdom," is over and has been replaced by consciousness with "skin, hair, claws, and teeth," all armed for dominance and power politics – where each nation and each individual are out "for themselves" to struggle for power. Suddenly, even semi-rational members of United States administration fell in line with Trump's nativism (not because he is one, but because nativist rhetoric attracts votes), stating that the world is not a global community but an arena where nations, non-governmental actors, and businesses engage and compete for advantage. This "advantage" is coupled with an unabashed admiration and mimicking of one, strong man leadership. The conservatives across the United States, with their "leader" at the head, are extoling the virtues of Putin, just as those of Xi Jinping of China, Orban of Hungary, Kaczynski of Poland, La Pen of France, the Czech Republic, and even the German left, and many others, forming a circle of like-minded "strong men" as the future. Conservative evangelicals are traveling to Russia to enjoy the moral climate where state and religion are united and moral virtues, such as suppression of gays and murder of those "liberals," including journalists, is the norm imposed by a strong man. Many are willing to abandon the European Union – already shown the way by Brexit. Under the guise of nationalism – "make America great," the West is surrendering its standards of democracy, openness, universal education, and civil society, and above all, freedom and equality.

The rhetoric of "America first" and the rest of the world (apart from dictatorships), including free press and speech, as enemy, is tweeted daily. All agreements must be rejected, from Davos through Southeast Asia, to North American Trade, and a global battle between "each man is for himself" has been extolled. Britain withdrew from the European Union, and autocrats began to show their nationalistic colors, with hints of breaking away from the universal rights, freedom and equality. The Davos global program has been credited with extending one market, one ecology, shared responsibility, coinciding with progress such that since 1981, when 44% of the world's population lived in extreme poverty, to today, when only 10% still need assistance. This globalism, once again coincided with the shift from liberal post-war system to neo-liberal arrangement, which not only dissolved the Soviet system, but brought China, even under its autocratic rule, into an open economy, international cooperation, with Chinese students and tourists flooding the West, to such an extent that, counter to Western trends of shrinking into self-imposed exclusiveness – Brexit, America first, France without Europe, autocracy with military adventures in Russia, Chinese president Xi Jinping proclaimed that global economy is the big ocean you cannot escape from – and we have learned to swim in it. In all respects, the American century was handed to China, allowing Xi to announce that China is moving to the central stage of the world. Our surrender is obvious when U.S. administration extols the "primacy of sovereignty," which is a traditional demand by dictators: "mind your own business" or "hands off the autocratic rulers." The Enlightenment on which U.S. was founded, as a rational democracy, is being handed over to Europe, which is also shifting to nationalistic "Endarkenment."

In the European Union, various countries are shifting toward their nationalisms which are counter to democracy, human rights, and a rule of law. In Poland, Hungary, the Czech Republic, the various nationalistic parties in France, England, Austria – just to name a few – regard democracy as enemy. (New York Times, April 8, 2018). While extolling equality, they all are dismantling institutions of freedom, whether it is free press, independent judiciary, and above all Western education. The latter is a primary institution which guarantees the presence of other institutions, including the public domain of freedom and equality. The attacks on Western education have become global, not only in the Middle East, but in China, Russia, and in the mentioned European nations. This is evident from the phenomenon spreading across Europe, under the term "identitarian." (*The Economist, March 31, 2018).* Promoting the primacy of "cultural" identity, premised on the notion that neo-liberal globalization, is destroying all cultural differences by the logic of "McDonalization," they are changing nationalistic activism. While being nationalistic, they are international, spilling over borders, from Scandinavia, Italy, France, Germany, and the United States. The activists call this movement "metapolitics," borrowed from an arch-Marxist, Antonio Grmamsci – indicating that Communism and current nationalisms of fascist types are closely linked. A Dutch writer, a while back, argued persuasively that dictatorial Soviet Union would be a paradise for Western conservatives (Peter Sloterdijk, 1987). The point should be obvious: neo-liberalism and its globalizing reach is no longer confronted with economic issues; it must face cultural claims which surpass economic needs. The "cultural wars" in the United States on both extremes – left and right – are not economic, to such an extent that both extremes coincide in the denial of the rights of the other to equality and freedom. This, of course, is the denial of the liberalism established after World War II. The mutual intolerance and rigteousness of each side is radically anti-Western, since Western civilization was founded on the recognition of human fallibility and thus a need for dialogue and correction of mistakes (Algis Mickunas, 2012).

While closing upon themselves, the nationalisms abandon international rules and tend to expand their power. Such is the case with Russia's invasion of Ukraine and rattling its military presence in Central Europe, and China's attempts to make the South China Sea, through which half of the world's commerce moves, into a China's lake, by creating artificial islands in definace of international law. And all the supporters of autocratic states no longer object to chemical warfare – the case in Syria and the murder of scores in Yemen. The butchery of peoples by holy warriors all over the world in the name of some ancient imagery depicted in some fairy tale is paraded as a right of a given culture to self-determination everywhere in the world. The most irrational racism by radically ignorant, swastika waving, half-naked images of the "future" of the Aryan race, who cheer every nonsensical noise coming from the leader, post signs that the age of Enlightenment is being replaced by the age of Endarkenment. Alternative facts, post-truth, and rewritten histories to suit the current nationalists have vast audiences, reaching into schools which deny the validity of Western universal education. And the latter is also being attacked in Western institutions of higher education, first, with intolerance, and second, with rejection of Western civilization; an offer of a course on this civilization was shut down by students at Stanford university as evil, colonialist and any other negative adjective, Eurocentric, homophobic, racist, immoral, despite the fact that it is the Western civilization which built such institutions allowing the young people the right to be ignorant. Media are replete with articles on "The Campus Culture Wars," yet it is in the West and no place else that sexual freedom was established, feminism flourished, without being stoned, hanged, or totally silenced. Certainly, young people could not reject proposed programs in China, the Middle East, Russia, and, perhaps soon, in the United States. To think, to engage in a dialogue as one major dimension of Western civilization, seems to be in decline. Dialogue, after all, means an admission that we are not omniscient, and only an assumption that we are results in claims by different views that each is absolute and all others are false and evil. There seems to be a gap which cannot be bridged.

The age of "Endarkenment" is best characterized by the return to an archaic – in its most primitive – mode of awareness. everything is "power." There are no other relationships, whether in the universe or human affairs, which are not power laden. Of course, no one, not even Nietzsche, with one of his theses that all life is will to power, has explicated the nature of power; even post-modern writers have fallen into this archaism by promoting the view that power is inherent even in the most innocent places – discourses. Now there are discursive struggles and confrontations, and since there are many discourses, it is an unavoidable war of all against all. Even under some remnants of democracy, there is a silent assumption that the elected servants of the public obtain positions of power. Such innocent slips as "which party got into power" tell of the primitive, archaic awareness. This is not to say that power is irrelevant, but to point out that the West had devised ways of managing its fury. Claims are made that liberalism failed, implying that Enlightenment and with it Western civilization failed, leading to the position that the option is autocracy and even theocracy.

The former has been in vogue since the building of great empires, from ancient Persia, through divine right of kings, to more rescent fascist, communist, and contemporary Russian promotion of Eurasian civilization, founded on one autocrat with military police controlling vast populations, backed by the Orthodox church with the autocrat as the head of state and church. As mentioned, Europe and the United States are showing signs of leaning in that direction, partially confirming the mentioned failure. The latter, theocracy, is in full bloom in the Middle East, with conservatives in compliance with the notion of the West being Judeo-Christian, needing a rejoining of Church and State. Of whatever ilk the church might be, it has a common agenda: Western secularism, with all its liberal institutions, laws, universal education, tolerance, autonomy, equality, is at the root of all evil. Abolition of secularism is identical with abolition of Western Enlightenment, liberalism, and a return to theocracy. Of course, such a return might open a holy war concerning which church is now in power – ending with the common practice: religious wars, already waged in the Middle East. It is then necessary to understand this Western civilization in principle in order to find a bulwark against all the contemporary power theories and their numerous variants in social, economic, political, and military domains. And it is the West, transgressing modern liberalism, which devised neo-liberalism, that provides a more encompassing, global, and locally relevant awareness about how freedom and equality can be rescued.

NEO-LIBERALISM

There are various readings of what neo-liberalism means. Some claim that the catalyst for neo-liberalism is an economic theoretician Heyeck (Wolfgang Streeck, 2014), while others point to "re-privatization" (Colin Grouch, 2011), and so on. To torture the reader with a litany of meanings would take volumes, resulting not in clarification, but in a Gordian knot. Hence, the attempt is to unravel the principles underlying neo-liberalism and how they relate to freedom and equality. The question is whether neo-liberalism can rescue freedom and equality from the nationalistic and autocratic, global attacks. While liberalism promotes international relationships and rules, including established laws, neo-liberalism "outruns" such rules, basically forged by governments. The latter were premised on stability and security and remained and still remain as one level of inner-international relationships. Meanwhile neo-liberalism thrives on temporal, dynamic relationships without borders. As we shall see from the "modal logic" of neo-liberalism, the first rule is *nothing is guaranteed, but anything is possible*. The latter term contains the understanding of multi-layered time systems which too are temporal. Such systems include most diverse factors in local-global relationships: economy, education, health, culture, ethics, ethnic identities, communication, and rights coupled with responsibilities. This suggests a second rule: *the modal logic is integrating, without assuming an "integral" whole*. It has been argued that each society is equivalent to a "life-world" which consists of "meaningful interconnections" (Algis Mickunas and Joseph Pilotta 2017). The life world is a network of meanings that point to each other. All the mentioned factors signify each other and can neither function nor be understood one without the others. Everything in this world comprises a normal view; everything seems clear and accustomed; questions and answers have a meaning despite controversial discussions. We are certain that a man has rights, that democracy disagrees with dictatorship, that our representatives serve us, notwithstanding their attempt to build their images of being a power that govern us, despite their corruption. We question them, complain about them, and, if necessary, we discard them for their dictatorial trends. We understand that work requires education, that culture has a tradition, that not all arts are allowed, that religion relates to peoples morals, and so on. Our life world, as the network of meanings, is our reality and even reflects a certain essence of what it is to be human. But we also surmise that not all life worlds are the same and that between them can be essential differences. However, their differences appear in reflection from another life world. Such a reflection is crucial for understanding the global appeal of neo-liberalism. First, a brief understanding of reflection, grounding neo-liberalism must be delimited.

Reflection is defined as a process applied on itself or upon processes of the same or a different kind. Such an application increases the function, efficiency, and management of these processes. Social processes, which become reflexive in this manner, are subtended by a selective process of informational management. This selective process is the reflexive dimension capable of managing a complexity of contents by reducing it to their proper spheres and by using mechanisms of simplification at increasing levels of abstraction. Thus, for example, the choice of commodities for the consumer is magnified through a monetary mechanism (the possibility to exchange possibilities). The same thing can happen with power when power is applied to power where the power of one or various processes is placed at the disposal of another process. The question that emerges is the following: what are the conditions for the possibility of the process of reflexivity? Everything must be understood temporally in a process and, hence, from a perspective of socio-historical variations and even radical breaks.

Any reflexivity presupposes as its condition the distinction between the real and the temporally possible or, as indicated above, the modalized. Thus, a particular social history does not vary only in terms of the presently given and selected facts, but also in terms of constitutive conditions of selectivity based on possibilities which are temporal. The insight into the selectivity of facts in any social process is a key to the constitution of the relationship between social facts, their structures, and the temporal horizons or possibilities. Thus the fundamental condition for possibility and for the selectivity of facts within a social process is temporality. This means that the condition for the possibility of a social system as a process is a modal generalization constituting the temporal horizons – in both temporal directions – of such a system. The consequence of such a modalized conception is that all selectivity and all delimitation of facts are based on a system's structure, conditioning in turn the horizon of possibilities from which events are selected. This selectivity is a process of reflexivity that it allows a distanciation from the present and a given location to its evaluation in terms of the various possibilities of the future. As a condition for the possibility of reflexivity, the temporal horizon offers a distanciation from the immersion into present facts and opens the various options in terms of which the present state of affairs could be evaluated. Yet it must be stressed that the options are not absolutely arbitrary. The social system itself, the life world of meaningful interconnections, may be used to reflect upon the horizon of possibilities and indicate the limitation of such a horizon: here emerge the socially possible and the socially impossible.

The temporal conditions for reflexivity are quite complex, although they can be managed by higher levels of reflexive inclusion. This means that modalized aspects can be again modalized under more inclusive possibilities and wider horizons. One can discuss the possibilities of reality and reality of possibilities or even possibility of possibilities, necessities, contingencies, and so on. The complexity of the temporal condition of reflexivity can be characterized in the following way. There can be a present future which must be distinguished from the future present even if only on the grounds that the present future contains more possibilities than is possible for future presents to become reality. One must also distinguish between future presents, present presents, and past presents, between the present of the past as history and the past present. If one begins with the two temporal horizons of the present, namely past and future which in each point can be seen as presents with their own pasts and futures with further possibilities of reiteration, then one begins to constitute the conditions for the possibility of all possible processes of reflexivity. This suggests that the indefinite modalizations of time horizons can be seen as temporal reflexivity in time. The immediate future can be reflected by a more remote future and both in turn by a still more remote and perhaps encompassing future yielding the structure for the reflexivity of possibilities in possibilities. This process is the condition for any distancing from the present facts and environment. It allows the postulation of the environment, be it the "material," "ideological," "juridical," "ethical," "ecological," "scientific," "created," "pragmatic-technical," "economic," and many possible others. The judgment of current events, environment, or facts is a judgement from a horizon of time and its possibilities requiring no hierarchical arrayment either of values or norms. This free-ranging reflection of time in time and possibilities in possibilities is the condition upon which all reflexive processes are based, be they economic, environmental, legal, cultural, educational, health, and so on.

Our most limited discussion of the conditions of reflexivity has opened the possibility to consider further the shift of the concept of theory, such as an economic explanation of social events in temporal sequence, to a concept of critical theory. First of all, it must be noted that within neo-liberal modal logic, theory has no longer a privileged status to be an extra-social, extra-historical or extra-temporal process, surveying events indifferently from a non-participating observer's stance. Theory, too, functions in society and its life world's temporal horizons, such that specific "explanation" changes the very events it attempts to explain. Hence, a theory must show how its explanation of events will influence such events, since such an explanation can be subsumed under reflexive process and its predictions either enhanced or thwarted. This means that a theory must correlate all factors and show how, in this correlation, some possibilities are realizable, others probable, and still others made impossible. For example, it must show how an economic capacity may be thwarted by a political ideology, a moral stance, or an economic misapplication; or how an economic capacity, yielding certain options, may become impossible due to technological incapacities, theological standards, or ethnic customs. At the same time, neo-liberal dynamics show the limits of the possibilities of a social system and delimit what changes must be instituted within certain social sub-systems to surpass the limitations as possibilities, yielding a reflection of time in time. Neo-liberal logic constitutes the most encompassing process of social reflexivity in historical and ultimately in the complexity of time horizons.

Due to its dynamic time reflexivity, and the possibility to take any current fact or a fact to be established, every possible construction, be it technological or cultural, ranges across more than one field. A changed computer logic is not only for computers, but for communication, production, political challenges, entertainment, education, various sciences, such that any of them can become a possibility for other ventures, equally open to become broader horizons, surpassing national boundaries, creation of groups of interest – spilling out onto the streets in protest – as "streetocracy," and all temporal. The creations of neo-liberal means – for example, smart instruments – take into account the specific local aspects, such as culture, education, language translations, opening such a local region toward global horizons of selectivity of novel options and social relationships. Modal logic, as a basis of neo-liberal practice, is also global and, as will be seen shortly, liberating and equalizing. Just taking its technical efficiency and promise of possibilities is an aspect of other life worlds. They see themselves in relationship to this efficiency, liberation from natural necessities and oppressive autocrats, and therefore part of their own self-understanding as different from this globalizing logic. The latter reflects the local inadequate and even unacceptable narrowness. This creates an internal tension within various cultures that constitute dual self-recognition wherein one still maintains his own cultural habits, yet also judges those habits in light of the global logic. This is the source of alienation and destruction of cultural self-identity. We still want to maintain cultural identity, but we also like to be "modern," to judge ourselves from the vantage point of images and possibilities not available in the local life world. This comprises a dual consciousness that frames the power struggles within various cultures. There are the modernizers who at the same time claim to be part of the local culture that want to transform that culture into an open, practically efficient, accessible to all, beneficial to individuals, liberating from ignorance, global life world, and wanting to maintain the uniqueness of the local culture.

A frequent solution to this tension is power. We witness the many confrontations between groups within given cultures that promote modernizations and at the same time fundamentalists and, as mentioned, current nationalists, who wish to close themselves in order to resist modernizations, and yet in order to do so, inevitably include global horizons. This means that a given culture is split into those who propagate the need to become globalized and modern, neo-liberal, and at the same time those who, while recognizing the necessity of this modernization, propose a battle against it as imposition of alien culture. This is the case of the Middle East. Yet, in every case, it seems that the reason for this power confrontation rests in the failure to understand the already-posited limit within which the globalizing process must function. This limit is the very requirement that the local cultures or their life worlds are made equivalent to all others by the globalizing logic, including the latter as one more option. What we have is a temporal horizon of possibilities for any life world to become present as unique among other unique life worlds, leading to the phrase "local-global." It is important to mention that the equivalence, whether cultural or individual, is not one of being the same, but the opposite – being unique precisely by being different from others: equivalence of differences – a reflective result.

The entire text – *A New Global Partnership* – is premised totally on "expectations" of what is possible – an open, temporal horizon which can be narrowed as to what is relevant and what is at present irrelevant or not yet possible in a specific location containing a life world of various interrelated factors, whether it is culture, education, health, or resources. This means that awareness is extended as a "past horizon" which is equally relevant since in some life worlds, the past horizon might be restricted to a specific tradition; its stories or eminent texts become equally relevant as to what shall be selected as significant from the future horizon. Some tightly-closed traditions decipher every future possibility on the basis of some past eminent text that restricts horizons of action to only certain possibilities. This is a way of saying that there is a selectivity of activities that are deemed to be proper and exclusion of those that are forbidden or irrelevant. This kind of time does not mean that humans make history – they are their history directly manifest in what they do, think, and build. The field of modal time is not connected causally, but "meaningfully" such that present events point to past and future events; i.e., they "signify" them, forming a "life-world." Even if events are past and causally no longer efficient, their significance is present not only as past but also as a factor in the horizon of what is possible. It can expand or contract the horizons by limiting and indeed closing the horizon to a narrow set of possibilities, or select and expand the horizon in terms of novelties. The current surge of nationalisms and their correlative theological associates constitute a dramatic narrowing of possibilities and thus diminishment of freedom. For a while, religions have been a private matter and are no longer mixed into political-public affairs; yet, more recently they reappeared in a virulent form not only in the Middle East, but globally. Their eminent texts from the past shifted toward the present social, political, educational, and cultural spheres, with a demand for future implementation of their edicts. Religions are entering political domain and shift the interpretation of laws, education, and morality, specifically when related to nationalisms. American white, conservative nationalists and evangelicals; Russian nationalists and the Orthodox church, with Putin as head of state and church; and all the above-mentioned European nationalists, mix their religion with public laws. This means that the narrowing down of horizons and open options is also a closure of freedom and abolition of equality both culturally, racially, and occupationally. This is a situation that discards economic priority in favor of cultural options – thus, the mentioned "cultural wars" instead of neo-liberal cultural equality. In this context, the understanding of the relationship between the temporal field and social structures should be obvious. Consequently, the dynamics of the temporal field of activity are limited by the social structure and its selected-selectable possibilities. Yet the modal logic of neo-liberalism is already global and any nation, which closes upon itself, cannot be immune to its horizons that make such closures a relic of the past. Moreover, the open horizons constitute the region of possibilities outside the ken of the social structure: in terms of the social structure, they are impossible. Yet precisely such "impossible-possibilities" define the limit of the social structure and its horizons and delineate the orientation for fundamental social changes and revolutions. The point is, "Globalization isn't going away" (Michael Schuman, 2018), including its foundation, global, local neo-liberalism.

THE NOMAD

What remains of the modern West, apart from the right to symbolic designs of identity, is the entire modern Western civilization of scientific enlightenment: everyone has equal rights, the latter are, in a practical domain, the right to obtain a profession through education, the right to engage in private enterprise, and the right to move to any region, either to join global business ventures or to offer one's technical expertise where the living conditions are more favorable. This is to say, the right to become detached from one's specific region and its symbolic designs of identity and to join the emergent nomadic civilization of experts, cultural creators, actors, tourists, whose various interests can be fulfilled as never before. This is not to say that such nomadic civilization is negative in any way; it is most attractive since it introduces continuous novelties in every area of social life: conveniences, medicines, travel, and communications, establishing new communities, and allowing the maintenance of ethnic ties around the globe. Indeed, the new communities can be among a great variety of interests and purposes or among the technical experts whose services are required at a moment's notice. In this global context, national and ethnic identities cannot depend on geographic locations or having national boundaries. With the global means of transportation, one can be home within a day. By virtue of gaining a technical set of skills, be they medical, computer, managerial, the members of a given nation/ethnicity become global and in their interests are more "at home" in the global community of professionals in their area of expertise than with the members of their traditional cultures. They attend international conferences, form associations and common projects, and are accepted everywhere. On the basis of the modal logic of neo-liberalism, the proliferation of technical disciplines is without limit; for example, chemistry, microchemistry, macrochemistry, biochemistry, genetic biochemistry, modeled by computer algorithms, etc., all the way to the changing "latest" and "improved" medications. The very language of such communities is not only discipline specific, but primarily interdisciplinary, involving participants from nations and continents. Of course, universal education is a prime ingredient, even if some autocracies, to their own and their citizens' detriment, including China, Russia, the Middle East and those mentioned in Europe and the United States, attempt to exclude such education, focusing only on narrow disciplines and invented cultural pride – worthless efforts for which the price is freedom and equality. While accepting all the scientific achievements of the modern West, based on enlightenment, the autocrats forget that without universal education – including critical and open thinking – their worlds will not endure.

Freedom and Equality

It is no longer adequate to claim the liberal thesis that individuals are autonomous and equal, since this claim is "out of this world;" freedom and equality depend on either the contraction or expansion of peoples' horizons, of opening up realizable possibilities or of closing them. As mentioned, the current nationalism and even racist ethnocentrism are closing the horizons for themselves and for others, not only limiting freedom, but also abolishing equality in the sense of denying equal access of everyone to participate in the possibilities which otherwise would be closed and create inequalities. Moreover, the freedom and equality are enriched by other life worlds, to be open to other communities and expand mutual horizons is an integrating in differences comprising mutual respect and understanding. One must only wonder what all the "intellectual critics" complain about when they attack neo-liberalism as having created a "consumer pop-culture," as if the latter prohibits any other culture to thrive – after all, operas, symphonies, and indigenous music, not only proliferate, but are accessible to vast populations either through media or tourism. Such critics want everyone to spill tears over Schubert, but not to enjoy jazz. What a morbid bunch. Neo-liberal modal logic provides an open world for anyone, including in economic terms. According to various pronouncements, one billion people got out of poverty, and the European Union is thinking of the tasks after or starting with the year 2015 that would eliminate poverty permanently. Of course, Europe cannot do it alone – it is a global task, even if Europe wants to play a leading role.

Neo-liberalism, meanwhile, produces directly perceptual, sensuous, bodily images, offering everyone the means to achieve equality in any corner drugstore, beauty parlor, grocery outlet, or fitness center. There is a global equalization in numerous domains: everyone can have similar foods, spices, and drinks, even similar looking clothing – despite differences in quality. To the anger of the mentioned critics, everyone is "enjoying" an apparent equality in terms of the socially-proliferated ideals and looks. "She looks like a million" and this despite the fact that she is working on an assembly line. The saturation of all domains with the images, tastes, sounds, and support groups lends technology a mystical power. Images of an ideal female, ideal male, ideal body, from toenails to hair, are proliferated for the "consumer." This is to say, ideology is no longer a matter of consciousness reflecting the material-economic or technical conditions, but is an inscription in the body, in the images, the passions, and desires appearing through the images and on the achieved body. The idealities of shared world of neo-liberalism are co-extensive with the daily discourse, daily imagery, mass media, sounds and tastes, architecture, popular arts carried by vast systems of circulation, thus making any art form accessible and "popular," and of course temporary.

It is sufficient to add some examples from India; it produces and exports countless technical experts to various continents and countries. They are diligent, industrious, and are nomadic. But they do not bring their home cultural symbols with them, and they do not adopt the symbolisms of the cultures in which they settle. They are detached experts and accept their assigned role by becoming consumers of the global standardized tastes, sounds, and looks advertised in all department stores, hair salons, fitness centers, and movies. They are no different in their wants as any other Westerner, and the men advertise for wives with specific properties:

Western looks, model-like figure, at least a master's degree, although a "real Indian woman." At the "cultural" level, they are as skin deep as any Westerner. Yet, they are most desired as technically superior in the areas of their expertise (Menon Rekha, 2010).

What remains of the liberal West, apart from the right to symbolic designs of identity, is the entire modern Western civilization of scientific and political enlightenments, now in the form of neo-liberalism: global intersection of various life-worlds, cultural mixing, conjunction of economic opportunities with education, health, international investment into the smallest ventures, and open horizons of selectivity. While everyone has equal rights, the latter are, in a practical domain: the right to obtain a profession through education, the right to engage in private enterprise, and the right to move to any region either to join global business ventures or to offer one's technical expertise where the living conditions are more favorable, or exhibit one's cultural uniqueness in the global arena. This is to say, the right to become detached from one's specific region and its symbolic designs of identity, and join the emergent nomadic civilization of detached experts, creators, and tourists, capable of visiting places where once only royalty could enter. This is not to say that such a nomadic civilization is negative in any way; it is most attractive since it introduces continuous novelties in every area of social life, forming new communications, and allowing the maintenance of ethnic ties around the globe. Indeed, the new communities can be among a great variety of interests and purposes, or more specifically among the technical experts, cultural stars, and investors, whose services are required at a moment's notice. In this global context, national and ethnic identities cannot depend on geographic locations, having national boundaries. With the global means of transportation, one can be home within a day, or speak face to face on Skype or the latest smartphone apps. One can "travel" the globe and "visit" commercial partners, cultural exhibits, and political events, or become a participant in "stratocracy." This participation and the expansion of its horizons is our concrete freedom and equality. What neo-liberalism promotes to date is a bold conjunction of universal education, global health, science, critical creativity, and open horizons. (*The Economist*,

April 28, 2019). A neo-liberal logic that discards ideological residua in favor of human life.

REFERENCES

"An Affordable Necessity" (*The Economist,* April 28, 2018, p. 45ff.)

Crouch, Colin (2011). *The Strange Non-Death of Neoliberalism.* (London: Cambridge).

Deleuze, Gilles, and Guattari, Felix (2009). *Anti-Oedipus: capitalism and schizophrenia,* Robert Hurley, tr. (New York: Penguin).

Deneen, Patrick (2017). *Why Liberalism Failed.* (Princeton: Yale University Press).

Hathaway, Oona and Shapiro, Scott (2017) *The Internationalists: How a Radical Plan to Outlaw War Remadew the World*. (New York: Simon and Schuster).

Horkheimer, Max, and Adorno, Theodor (2002). *Dialectic of Enlightenment,* G.S. Noerr ed., E. Jephcott, tr. (Stanford: Stanford University Press).

Jessop, Bob and Ngai-Ling, Sum (2006). *Beyond the Regulation Approach.* (Northampton, MA: Edward Elgar).

Mickunas, Algis (2012). *The Divine Complex and Free Thinking.* (Chesterhill, N.J. Hampton Press).

Mickunas, Algis with Pilotta, Joseph (2017). *Lived World of Social Theory and Method.* (New York: Nova Science Publications).

New York Times, April 10, 2018.

Schuman, Michael (2018). "Globalization Isn't Going Away" in *Bloomberg Businessweek,* March 19, 2018.

Sloterdijk, Peter (1987). *Critique of Cynical Reason.* Michael Eldred tr. (Mineapolis: University of Minnesota Press).

Streeck, Wolfgang (2014). *New Left Review,* 87. May/June, 2014.

"White, right and pretentious," *The Economist,* March 31, 2018.

BIOGRAPHICAL SKETCH

Algis Mickunas

Affiliation: Prof. Emeritus, Ohio University; Prof. of Philosophy at 3 universities in Lithuania.

Education:
Illinois Institute of Technology, 1955-1959, BS
DePaul University, Chicago, 1959-1963, BA
DePaul University, Chicago, 1963-1964, MA
Cologne University, Germany, 1964-1965,
Freiburg University, Germany, 1965-1966,
University of Chicago, 1966-1967,
Emory University, Atlanta, 1967-1969, PhD

Business Address: Department of Philosophy, Ohio University, Athens, OH, 45701, USA

Professional Appointments:
Short seminars on semiotics and comparative studies – from Guatemala through Freiburg.
Vytautas Magnas University Professor, 2007-2018.
Universidad Rafael Landivar, Guatemala, 2001-2009, yearly seminars on globalization.
Klaipeda University, Visiting Professor, 1995-1998.
Vilnius University, Visiting Professor, 2006, 2011, 2014, 2016.
Ohio University, Athens, Ohio, Professor of Philosophy, 1986-present
Ohio University, Athens, Ohio, Associate Professor of Philosophy, 1974-1984
Lynchburg College, Lynchburg, Virginia, East Distinguished Visiting Professor, 1980-1981
Ohio University, Athens, Ohio, Assistant Professor of Philosophy, 1969-1974

Emory University, Atlanta, Georgia, Instructor, 1968-1969

Honors:

Appointed to the Lithuanian Academy of Science, 2008.
Received Honorary Doctor Degree from Klaipeda University, Lithuania, 2000.
Received Honorary Doctor Degree in Humanities, Universidad Rafael Landivar, Guatemala, 2009.
Received Honorary Doctorate Degree, Vilnius University, 2011.
Received Honorary Doctorate Degree, Mykolas Romeris University, 2012.

Publications from the Last 3 years:

Books

Mickunas, Algis & Pilotta, J., *Lived World of Social Theory and Method*. New York: Nova Science Publishers, 2017.
Mickunas, Algis, *Kosminė Sąmonė* [*Cosmic Consciousness*]. Vilnius: VU Leidykla, 2017.
Mickunas, Algis, *The West and the Others*. Riga: Lambert Academic Publishers, 2018.
Mickunas, Algis, *From Zen to Phenomenology*. New York: Nova Science Publishers, 2018.
Mickunas, Algis, *Before the Ad Image: Body Memory in Motion*. New York: Nova Science Publishers, 2018.
Mickunas, Algis. *Istorija – Kalba – Suvokimas* [*History – Language – Awareness*]. VU Leidykla, 2019.
Mickunas, Algis. *Anarchies in Collision*. New York: Nova Science Publishers, 2019.

Articles

Mickunas, Algis. "The Different Other and Dialogue." In: *Coactivity: Philosophy, Communication,* 2016, Vol. 24, No. 1, 3-13.

Mickunas, Algis, "Resistance to Western Popular and Pop-Culture in India. In: *Coactivity: Philosophy, Communication,* 2017, Vol. 25, No. 1, 48-62.

Mickunas, Algis, "Polycentric Awareness and Communication. In: *The Journal of Communication and Religion,* Vol. 40, No. 3, 2017.

Mickunas, Algis, "Transcendental Ground of Intrinsic Worth in Russian Literature. In: *Investigatciones Fenomenologicas,* Vol. 7, Jesus Diax & Maria-Luz Pinta-Finaranda, eds. Madrid: Sefe, 2018.

Mickunas, Algis, "William Dilthey: Artistic Imagination. In: *An Encyclopedia of Communication Ethics: Goods in Contention,* Ronald C. Arnett, ed. New York: Peter Lang, 2018, p. 131-136.

Mickunas, Algis, "Edmund Husserl: To the Things Themselves. In: *An Encyclopedia of Communication Ethics: Goods in Contention.* Ronald C. Arnett, ed. New York: Peter Lang, 2018, p. 238-242.

In: Neoliberalism
Editor: Travis Graham

ISBN: 978-1-53616-014-7
© 2019 Nova Science Publishers, Inc.

Chapter 2

THE NEOLIBERAL AGENDA IN HIGHER EDUCATIONAL INSTITUTIONS: PERSPECTIVES, IMPACTS AND THE WAY FORWARD

Gifty Oforiwaa Gyamera, PhD*
Ghana Institute of Management and Public Administration (GIMPA), Accra, Ghana

ABSTRACT

For the past few decades, neoliberalism has become a dominant ideology influencing governmental and institutional policies and practices across the world. It has transcended the political, economic, cultural and social contexts.

Ghana, as a country, has not been insulated from the tentacles and influences of neoliberalism. Recently, neoliberalism has been firmly implanted and has permeating various institutions including higher education. This emphasis on neoliberalism is derived from the capitalist

---

* Corresponding Author's E-mail: ogyamera@gimpa.edu.gh.

ideology the country was forced to adopt in the 80's due to harsh economic conditions. This study draws on data on neoliberal discourses and practices in universities in Ghana. It situates neoliberalism in a historical framework and looks at how it is perceived and manifested in various aspects of the universities, the impact and the way forward.

Initial findings of the study suggest that many of the reforms which have occurred in the universities, particularly over the past two decades, were mainly informed by neoliberal ideologies. These reforms influenced varied aspects of the universities including infrastructural development, curriculum changes, expectations and demands of academics and administrators and restructuring of departments. The values, structures and processes of the private sector have been adopted by the universities. A vital element is an emphasis on 'performance' measured by quantitative outcomes. The mandates of the universities appear to have changed from knowledge creation and dissemination to production of marketable skills and promoting of entrepreneurship. All the universities are engaged in enterprising activities, competition and promoting their brand. Whilst there are some positive implications including improved infrastructural development, the disadvantages appear overwhelming. Both academics and administrators are confronted with many challenges including individualism, job insecurity and excessive stress. Inequalities and meritocracy have become the norm. In spite of these challenges, little is being done to resist the neoliberal ideologies. Both academics, administrators and senior management have accepted its performativity expectations. Everyone strives to fulfill them.

I argue for the need of academia to resist neoliberal ideologies as the dominant ideology governing universities. There should be much research into the impact of neoliberalism on higher educational institutions.

Keywords: neoliberalism, higher education, quality assurance, academic experiences, curriculum

INTRODUCTION

For the past few decades, neoliberalism has become a dominant ideology influencing governmental and institutional policies and practices across the world. As a concept, it involves promotion of the free market of economic exchange and reduction of state and government interference

(Block, 2018: Giroux, 2015). Its ideologies have transcended the political, economic, cultural and social (Block, 2018: Norris, 2019) spanning across the global, national, state, local and institutional levels. It has become the very essence of existence for both individuals and organisations and all activities are organized in relation to the market model. Expectedly, though in many ways undesirable, neoliberal ideologies have pervaded higher educational institutions globally.

Since the 1980s, neoliberalism has been firmly implanted in Ghana and has permeating various institutions including higher education. Its ideologies have gradually but steadily seeped into the core fabric of high educational systems in the country. It has impacted the structures, governance, policies and practices of the institutions and appears to define the very existence of high education in Ghana.

In spite of the pervasiveness of neoliberalism in the universities, both faculty and administrators appear to know little about this concept. Neoliberal policies and practices are not only perceived as the new common sense, it is highly sought after and university leaders who exhibit neoliberal principles are perceived as heroes and leaders worth emulating.

This chapter draws on data on neoliberal discourses and practices in universities in Ghana. It situates neoliberalism in a historical framework and looks at how it is perceived and manifested in various aspects of the universities, the impact on particularly, young faculty, and the way forward. The paper aims to develop understandings about the concept in order to enable universities to develop processes and practices that are more context sensitive. It argues for universities to make careful reflections on neoliberalism and its ramifications on higher education. It recommends strategies including creation of awareness of the ramification of neoliberal ideologies on particularly young academics, mentoring, and provision of resources and promotion of a sense of belonging to address some of the negative impacts.

The paper will be in four sections. The first provides a brief introduction and literature review of the study including the historical background of neoliberalism in Ghana, the second explains the methodology of the research, the third presents the findings and discussions whilst the fourth provides recommendations and conclusions. It is significant to note that literature on neoliberalism in Ghana is very limited. This paper therefore draws heavily on literature from mainly Western and also other African contexts.

NEOLIBERALISM AS A CONCEPT

Neoliberalism, as a popular concept, has many definitions and interpretations. One of the most popular definitions is by Harvey who perceives it as 'a theory of political economic practices that proposes that human wellbeing can best be advanced by liberating individual entrepreneurial freedoms and skills within an institutional framework characterized by strong private property rights, free markets and free trade' (2005, 2). Kotz (2015, 9) sees it as an institutionalised capitalism which has gradually emerged as a dominant form of economic and social regulations. Though, there are different definitions and interpretations of neoliberalism, a common trend seems to manifest in all the definitions. It is an agenda which promotes the market, regulation of the economy and minimal state intervention. In its extreme form, neoliberalism is based on the premise that 'the liberalisation of markets, including the free flow of capital, goods, people, knowledge and ideas holds the promise of economic rewards and overall increases in welfare (Desjardins 2013, 185).

Characteristics, Benefits and Challenges of Neoliberalism

Neoliberalism has many forms and a number of characteristics (Giroux, 2014; Windle, 2019). It is perceived as an economic and political scheme involving an ideology, mode of governance, policy and form of public pedagogy (Giroux, 2014). For instance, as an ideology, it regards profit making as the crux of democracy, emphasises consumption as the core of citizenship, and endorses the belief that the market can solve all problems. The market is also a conduit for organizing all social relations. It underscores self-help and responsibility of the individual. As a mode of governance, "it produces identities, subjects, and ways of life driven by a survival of the fittest ethic, grounded in the idea of the free, possessive individual, and committed to the right of ruling groups and institutions to accrue wealth removed from matters of ethics and social costs" (Giroux, 2014, par. one). Neoliberal principles emphasise open markets, decreased public spending and reduced state intervention in the market (Torres, 2011, 184).

Neoliberalism could be perceived as a very controversial concept with varied criticisms and applause. Along a continuum, there are those perceptions at the extreme ends: the 'liberal dream' and the 'commodified' nightmare. The liberal dream endorses the dominance of the market as beneficial whilst the commodified nightmare emphasises the destructive aspect of the market (Fourcode and Healy, 2007). Espousers of neolieberalism believe that the market is the best regulator and creates maximum wealth. According to them, competition provides the best means for global economic growth and prosperity which immensely benefits both states and individuals (Harman, 2008). According to critics however, among the many challenges, neoliberalism erodes social and public life (Giroux 2015) and restores class power. Again, as organisations and institutions become market entities, workers are perceived as individual enterprises and forced to work in competitive environments. Inequalities are perceived and enhanced as a natural order (Dardot & Laval, 2013). In all the challenges, the individual, and not the society, is blamed for these inequalities (Desjardins 2013).

In spite of these misgivings, almost every country has embarked on neoliberal agendas, sometimes voluntarily and sometimes through coercive pressures (Torres, 2011).

Emergence of the "Entrepreneur" University

Institutions of higher education have not escaped the tentacles of neoliberalism (Torres and Jones, 2013). There is now the emergence of neoliberal universities which is modeled after corporate bodies. It is characterized by sustained market-like behaviour and governance (Ibid) including 'instrumental reasoning...competitiveness, excellence and performance' (Ibid, 347). Over a decade now, as argued by many scholars and researchers, the economics, structure, purpose and priorities of higher education including faculty and students' identity have been reformed to more conform to neoliberal practices and ideology (e.g., Giroux, 2015). Neoliberalism has created a new common sense that has percolated into all public and private institutions and thus, despite their own autonomy, into institutions of higher education' (Harris, 2011, 183). For instance, universities all over the world now seem engrossed in how to restructure the curriculum to attract funding from both national and international students.

These corporate practices also include advertisement and election of Vice Chancellors, privatisation of subjects and embarking on business activities in the universities (Munene, 2007). Others are absence of collegial decision making and limited access to information base on which decisions can be made. Many decisions are now made in secret and administrators 'now reading management books written for the corporate world, which explain how managers can bring about reforms quickly' (Currie et al. 2002, 5).

There is what Torres and Jones describe as 'an assault on education and knowledge...' (2013, 180). Knowledge is instrumentalised to serve 'purely the purposes of economic growth, often at the expense of democracy, justice or fairness' (Ibid).

Many academics have expressed concern about the negative impact of neoliberal ideologies in higher education (e.g., Gyamera and Burke, 2017). However, despite the concerns it is very difficult for universities and academics to ignore the market trend because their survival depends on following the trend (Giroux, 2015). The market trends are parameters set by funding agencies like the World Bank who may pressurise the universities to adopt these trends. Some of the pressures can be mild or very direct and most often the adoption of their programmes is the basis for funding. Thus, many universities in the developing countries are forced to embark on such strategies which appear to make them more susceptible to exploitation.

THE HISTORICAL BACKGROUND OF NEOLIBERALISM IN GHANA

Neoliberalism became entrenched in Ghana's politics in the early 80s when intense negative economic conditions including very high inflation and lack of foreign exchange confronting the nation forced ex-President John Jerry Rawlings' military government, the Provisional National Defense Council (PNDC), to make a ' U-turn' from its socialist stand to 'Pro-West liberal policies' in April, 1983 (Ibid). This decision also led to the adoption of structural adjustment programmes (SAP). Among others, SAPs aimed at addressing budget deficits, balance of payment (BOP) deficits and the resulting debt problem through boosting exports, discouraging imports and attracting foreign investment (Omtzigt, 2008). There was a strong alignment to the wave of market including deregulation, privatization, and welfare-state withdrawal in the 80s and 90s.

The 'PNDC demonstrated unprecedented and relentless pursuit of liberal economic policies after its initial socialist posturing had been abandoned' (Boafo-Arthur, 2007, 7). In 1992, the country adopted democratic governance as a condition of the Structural Adjustment Progamme (SAP) marking the 'beginning of a serious attempt by Ghana to enthrone the liberal state in all its ramifications.' (Ibid, 227). The PNDC, which now changed its name to the National Democratic Congress (NDC), but led by former President Rawlings, contested the election that year and won. Thus the policies pursued under the previous government continued.

However, by 2000, Ghana was caught 'in a poverty/debt-trap and became extremely aid- dependent' (Bank of Ghana, n.d., 4). This challenge and a general discontentment of the NDC government led to its defeat in a general election conducted in December 2000 and coming into power, the

New Patriotic Party (NPP). In 2001, on the assumption of office as the President of Ghana, John Agyekum Kuffor of the New Patriotic Party (NPP) opted for debt relief under the Highly Indebted Poor Countries (HIPC) Initiative of the World Bank and IMF. The HIPC initiative adopted by the government relieved Ghana of its public debt substantially (World Bank, n.d.). He however continued relentlessly with the SAP and thus had to continue with its numerous conditions including devaluing the currency, abolishing price controls and import and export quotas, and redefining the role of the state so that the state does not expand its roles. Others included adopting monetary and fiscal policies such as ensuring a balance in the budget, and the government not required to resort to printing money (Omtzigt, 2008). The country also adopted the Ghana Poverty Reduction Strategy (GPRS 1) policy framework. The New Patriotic Party was defeated in 2008 general elections, ushering back into power, the National Democratic Congress (NDC).

The National Democratic Congress was in power from 2008 to 2016 under two different leaders, the late John Atta Mills (2008-2012) and John Dramani Mahama (2012- 2016). They also blazed the footsteps of their predecessors, in terms of dedication to neoliberal principles. Presently, the NPP has been back in power since January, 2017 and continuing the path of neoliberalism with its varied ramifications on higher education.

METHODOLOGY

Qualitative methodology framed this research and it involved two public universities in Ghana. I adopted a qualitative method for this research because it allows understanding of complex realities as well as the meaning of actions in a given context. It enhances deeper insight towards the respondent's beliefs, attitudes, or situation (Shakouri, 2014). This approach gave participants the opportunity to bring out their feelings, understandings, perceptions and rationales of neoliberal ideologies and the varied ways in which universities are responding to it. In the midst of silence participants were empowered by this methodology to share their stories and to hear their own voices (Creswell, 2007, 40).

Convenience sampling was used to select the institutions based on feasibility. Recently, all public universities have embarked on dramatic changes to meet international and national demands often adopting what could be interpreted as neoliberal ideologies (universities' websites). There was therefore an implication that I will be able to derive data from any of the universities without purposively focussing on particular ones. Besides this is an explorative research to determine the extent of neoliberal activities in the universities so any of university could have be chosen to explore impact on data to be acquired.

At each university, I used purposive sampling to select key university managers and faculty members. University managers included deans of schools/faculties and heads of departments. These participants selected were very key in providing pivotal information on neoliberal ideologies in the universities. The academics involved both senior and junior academics. Senior members is defined as members with PhDs and who are at the level of senior lecturer and above. Junior faculties are defined as academics with or without PhDs and who are at the rank of a lecturer and below. One key policy maker of tertiary education at the national level was also interviewed. Though I involved both senior and junior members, in this paper, I will focus on the responses of junior academics. As indicated by Archer (2008), with the emergence of the neoliberal universities, most studies have focused on senior academics and their responses to this new concept. There is the need to devout a space to explore the perception of young academics.

The instruments I chose for this research were mainly interviews and documentary analyses. I also drew heavily on my experience as a student, an academic and a researcher in three key universities in Ghana. The interview guide focused on how participants understand the concept of neoliberalism, whether they think it important and why, the strategies that have been initiated and implemented in response to neoliberalism and its impact on faculty. The participants were evenly distributed across institutions. At each university, 15 individuals were interviewed. In total,

30 individual interviews were conducted. Strategic and mission reports, along with university handbooks were some of the documents. I used. The themes for gathering my data were greatly influenced by the literature.

Key writers whom I drew upon included Brooks (2018), Harris (2011), Giroux (2015; 2014) and Torres and Jones (2013). The data was coded and categorised to reveal patterns and to identify emerging themes and domains (Given 2008). A key aspect of the categorisation was to look for internal and external integrity (Given 2008). This I did by making sure that the categories richly reflected the data to enhance internal external integrity (Ibid). The ethical issues concerned voluntary informed consent, access, confidentiality, anonymity, the protection of participants from physical and emotional discomfort and/or harm and the right to privacy as stipulated by the British Educational Research Association (2004). Participants were assured of confidentiality, anonymity and were assured of their right to opt out of the study or refuse to answer particular questions if they are uncomfortable to answer.

FINDINGS AND DISCUSSIONS

This section presents the initial findings and discussions. It will look at some manifestations of neoliberal influences and its impact on young academics.

Neoliberal Influences on Higher Education

The findings indicated that neoliberalism has indeed pervaded the institutions influencing their policies and practices impacting on varied aspects including administrative, research and teaching and learning outcomes. These influences have emanated both from the national level and institutional levels.

National Level

At the national level, the introduction of neoliberal ideologies has resulted in two key educational reforms: the 1987 and 2007 educational reforms. Although, since Ghana attained independence in March, 1957, there have been various reviews and reforms of the education system including the 1966, 1974, 1993 and 2002 (Tonah, 2009), the 1987 and 2007 reforms particularly reflected the neoliberal policies adopted by the Government as the genesis of these reforms could be traced to structural adjustment programmes adopted by the government in 1983. It is significant to emphasize that although these reforms did not focus exclusively on higher education, they brought some changes to these institutions. I will give a brief highlight on some key impacts of the 1987 and 2007 impact on higher education

1987 Educational Reform

Whilst the reform changed the structure and content of primary and secondary education (Girdwood, 1999) it also sought to remedy the deteriorated conditions of higher education, particularly, the universities. It particularly set out to control the quality and relevance of teaching, learning and curriculum within a self-regulatory framework (WP, 2). Consequently, many governmental bodies including the National Council for Tertiary Education (NCTE) and the National Accreditation Board (NAB) were established to assess programmes offered in these institutions (Girdwood, 1999).

Policies including cuts in government subventions, cost sharing, wealth creation, and implementation of packages of deep austerity measures in an effort to balance national budgets were introduced. There were also policies on efficiency and financial appropriation (Girdwood, 1999). Though the reform was broad and visionary various challenges including the failure of both the University Regulatory Council (URC) and policy-makers, to define 'academic quality' as well as the methodology to be used to ensure quality, little clarifications on teaching aims, objectives and modalities of delivery limited its effectiveness (Ibid). Other challenges related to administration and the management of education… and sustainable financing of the whole tertiary education sector (White paper 2007, 1.1). This led to the development of the 2007 educational reforms.

The 2007 Educational Reform

In 2007, another educational reform was introduced to ensure the 'formation of well-balanced individuals with the requisite knowledge, skills, values, aptitudes and attitudes to become functional and productive' (White Paper on Educational Reforms, 2007, 5.0). In terms of tertiary education, it particularly reaffirmed neoliberal principles in the institutions. There was an emphasis on research and postgraduate programmes and it aimed to enhance access, quality, equity and relevance to meet the needs of a modern economy. As part of addressing the financial challenges, all tertiary institutions were required to 'reinforce their links with the private sector economy, including industry... (White paper on Educational Reforms, 2007, 20). Diversification strategies and cost-sharing arrangements were emphasised.

Institutional Levels

At the institutional levels, the effects of these reforms and the need to follow global dictates led to various strategic reforms and plans in the last decade which are explained in the next session. In his report about changes that have occurred in the university within his tenure, the then Vice-Chancellor of one of the universities stated in a report of his tenure as the Vice Chancellor 'There exists a global trend among institutions of higher learning to reform and restructure in order to enhance their efficiency and effectiveness in meeting the demands of the global world. The University of ... cannot be left out (Report, 2009, 5).

Perception about the Infiltration of Neoliberalism in the Universities

Though neoliberal ideologies, policies and practices are rife in the universities, the initial findings suggest that the majority of participants had limited knowledge about neoliberalism as a concept, and its influences in the universities and thus did not attribute many of the new happenings to it. All participants had perceived the occurrences as natural to how the universities must actually operate. And in many ways, these practices are mirrored by academics in Western universities, which many universities in non-Western countries try unending to emulate. Some of the participants were however quick to relate neoliberalism to capitalism which enhanced their understanding about the neoliberal ideology.

Though this is an initial finding, the responses could be reflective of the larger population and an indication why few voices, if any, has written or spoken about the impact of neoliberalism in the universities. Both at the national and institutional levels, few voices seem to be challenging the takeover of the neoliberal agenda.

This limited criticism, however, could be also be attributed to the dominant neoliberal institutional culture where academics hardly criticize government or institutional managers for fear of being tagged and falling out of favour of these authorities. In the context of the silence, neoliberal ideologies continue to reign in the universities. The next session explain some of the impacts of neoliberal ideologies in the institutions.

Manifestations of Neoliberalism in the Universities

The responses indicated that neoliberalism, as a concept is manifested in varied ways including wealth creation, changes in curriculum (these changes were the focus of a previous paper), administrative structures, expectations and demands on faculty.

Wealth Creation

The urgency to become entrepreneurial and to generate wealth has become an underlying goal in the universities (Gyamera and Burke, 2018; Gyamera, 2017). In Ghana, this need has exacerbated with the dwindling of Government funding vis a vis the needs of universities. Both universities have prioritized revenue generation and have initiated efforts to be enterprising. The universities' commitment to be fully entrepreneurial become more manifest and radical when in 2000, there was a national directive for institutions and organisations to prioritise wealth creation (Asante, 2012, 9). The 2007 Educational Reforms reinforced this directive and universities were particularly admonished to emphasise cost-sharing among other funding diversification strategies.

Subsequently, the universities have become increasingly reliant on private sources of funding and are engaged in numerous private ventures including establishment of, hotels, guest houses, consultancy services and sellable programmes. In one of the universities, for instance, almost every single School has a guest house. This is in addition to numerous hostels to accommodate students, particularly international students with high prices.

Changes of Administrative Structures

To enhance the wealth creation activities, there were changes in names of departments, while some were merged, all to reflect corporate bodies. In both universities for instance, there are now Human Resource departments instead of Personnel offices. There are also Corporate Affairs departments which are also engaged in varied corporate activities reflecting the name. One of the respondents, in expressing his disagreement with some of these changes explained:

> Personally...I think that we are trying to, we are masquerading as something we are not. We are not a corporate world. Of course we can borrow some but I don't think that we should have a whole sale of universities as a corporate bodies. Sometimes it even sounds ridiculous and trivial that suddenly something that used to be called personnel office is called personnel office of the human resource something...I don't personally agree that that is the way we should go (Dean and a Professor).

However, such corporate terminologies and practices have become the norm in each of the universities as they provide the basis for their wealth creation.

Market Driven Curriculum

Neoliberal policies and ideas are equally shaping curriculum development in the universities. It appears each programme developed is influenced by the commodification, commercialization, and marketization logic. There is overemphasis on economic outcomes (Gyamera and Burke,

2017) with a sustained gaze on what the universities could gain economically.

In terms of programmes, the universities have expanded the scope of teaching, learning and research to respond to perceived global and national demands. A major change to this effect is the expansion of their programmes to include programmes different from their mandates (Gyamera and Burke, 2017). There have also been shifts in target population. For instance, one of the universities whose core mandate was to offer postgraduate programmes to public servants has now expanded to include undergraduate students.

The institutions have also developed varied normal and executive programmes demanded by the market. Various customised programmes have been developed for key stakeholders and individuals in key sectors of the economy. The emphasis is not only about the programmes, various strategies have been implemented to enhance quality in the teaching-learning activities.

Quality Related Strategies

To enhance the quality of their lecturers, there is now a policy in both universities requiring all lecturers to hold PhD degrees. Consequently, in most departments there is a mandatory minimum entry point of PhD for all lecturers to teach in the universities. To facilitate this policy, many members of faculty are sent abroad to do their PhD study.

The neoliberal agenda has equally impacted on grading systems. Over the last decade, both universities have changed their grading systems upwards. With the new policy, students need to get 80 percent and above to get an A, 75-79 percent to get a B+ and 70-74 percent to get a B. This is unlike earlier years when students needed to get 70 percent and above to get an A.

To ensure that academic programmes meet their goals, the universities have established centres of quality assurance directed by Professors. The Centres have major roles in assessing and evaluating lecturers, programmes, methods of teaching and examinations. Students are also given the opportunity to assess lecturers on their performance in the lecture rooms.

As participants indicated, major reason for effecting these curriculum changes in the universities is to compete for students, particularly, international students. The changes are also to enhance employment opportunities of students both at home and abroad. At times, it appears to go beyond employment to simply the financial gains.

Expectations of Faculty

The neoliberal changes have affected the roles, work and identities of academics (Archer, 2008: Collins, 2017). Similar to what is happening globally and as indicated by participants, faculty members in the universities are now perceived as 'knowledge workers' and expected to be 'tireless, compliant and expendable' in every demand. Beyond their core duties of research, teaching and community service, they are expected to be administrators, marketers of the institutions, fund raisers, peer assessors and student counsellors and advisors (Oleksiyenko, 2018, 193).

Publication and Research

Faculty are expected to publish in categorised journals most of which are 'reputable' international journals. Most African journals are 'C' or 'D' rated and thus not particularly considered. The majority of participants expressed worry about this typified by these responses:

> ...there are also specifics publication outlets that we have to publish with which I think is more of the foreign ones. And I think there should be a balance because with the foreign ones if they are concentrating on the A, B and whatsoever, it takes a lot of time... (Young academic)

> And where they want you to publish, sometimes, your whole life you cannot publish there (Young academic).

Additionally, it has become mandatory for faculty members seeking promotion above senior lectureship to be experts in raising funds. They should have acquired a certain amount of funding for the university. Thus faculty members are obediently supposed to devout ever-increasing time to exploring and planning funding opportunities and strategies, writing proposals and reports and promoting the institutions (DeSouza, 2011). Faculty members' worth appear to be tied to monetary values (Cannella & Koro-Ljungberg, 2017, 156).

Surveillance

Neoliberal universities tend to increase surveillance which contributes to the intensification of academics' workload (e.g., Oleksiyenko, 2018). Various checks have been put in place to ensure that academics do not relegate any of their expected roles to the background. For instance, at the first university, faculty members are subjected to religiously, non-negotiable student assessment. At the time of writing, peer review has also been introduced to augment assessment of faculty members.

Concerning its challenges some of the respondents indicated that they do not even think students understand what they are tasked and required to do. As one participant explained:

> The problem I have with students reviewing our work and giving marks to what we do is the fact that some… I do not know if some of the students really understand what they tick because for instance, I give them the content/course outline, everything is there, I make photocopies and give to students. Sometimes I send them through the class reps so that they can distribute … and when they were ticking they said I did not give any course outline.

I share similar experiences as an academics, and have complained about this issue severally. Similar to the response above, I give course outline to students and explain every detail but during evaluation, many will indicate that they did not receive and did not understand the course outline. It appears students just tick boxes. Mostly, this become frustrating to academics.

Emphasis on Economic Efficiency

To enhance wealth creation there is a critical emphasis on economic efficiency. Managers of universities who are able to exhibit this 'coveted' skill are hailed. A former Vice-Chancellor in one of the universities became very popular and is almost considered a legend in the landscape of higher educational management in Ghana because he introduced most of the neoliberal ideologies in this institutions. He emphasised marketization of programmes. It has also been said so many times by many employees how he could solely withdraw an employee's appointment or recruit another at any moment he deemed fit. At a particular period, he removed over 120 staff who he thought were redundant.

Contract of Lecturers

One key tool to enhance efficiency is the introduction of the contract system, similar to what is happening globally. Both universities practice the contract system though they have different renewal periods. In one of the universities, newly recruited PhD faculty members are given six year contract whilst those with Mphil are given three year contract during which they must be promotable. If at the end of the contract a faculty member is not promotable, his contract is not renewed.

The Rule of Segregation

Another manifestation of neoliberal ideologies is the 'rule of segregation' (Oleksiyenko, 2018). In both universities there appears to be a deep segregation between managers of universities, senior members and junior members as reflected by the responses below:

> So that neoliberalism has created a lot of problems in higher education, teared relationship, them and us... those who are there and those who are here and this kind of separation creates a lot of problems, exclusion problems... to exclude others and make themselves the superior and other (Young academic)

> It is still that bottom-up approach. Is it not precisely what was said, that they are not going to give chances to those whose noses are

running...so at (Mentions the Institution) it is still that teared relationship because management feel they are the ones at the top and lecturers, apart from senior lecturers who have some managerial roles allocated to them at a certain point, all others are nothing... which is a very sad situation so I think the relationship between management and lecturers still balls down to us and them.. They are here we are there and that to me suppresses and delegates lecturers to an inferior position

The distinction between the different ranks of senior members involving lecturers, senior lecturers and professors is equally working mentioning. A lecturer is perceived as having very little to offer the universities.

I think even amongst the lecturers, there is always this kind of people saying, if you are a lecturer then you are low there...when that becomes... there is always this tension when it comes to people contributing to their ideas in terms of how to even move the department forward and all that. I think that no matter your position, whether you are a lecturer, a senior lecturer or a professor, we should all see ourselves as one so that people will feel at home (Young academic)

In one of the universities, respondents pointed out how even during social and formal events of the university, the segregation is glaringly pursued with seating arrangement with management seated as a group in one place, senior members in different groups and junior members in another set of groups. This segregation is reflected in decision making processes in the universities.

Limited Shared Governance
The emphasis on segregated rule and the need to enhance perceived efficiency have also resulted in limited shared governance. The age-long system of collegiality appears not to be existing in the universities. Responses confirmed hierarchical models of decision making has now become the norm with decision making limited to some few individuals.

The implication here is that excluded individuals are in a subtle and in some cases conspicuously made to think and assume that their views and ideas are not important nor relevant and that only few individuals could make effective and efficient decisions for the institutions. One participant explained:

> The pursuant of this capitalism idea has given too much authority to some few people who run the institution in lieu of their personal interest and that really subjects other members of the community to risk which makes them feel un-belonged and therefore end up giving their minimum best.

Such segregations depict what Oleksiyenko, (2018) described as a 'factory model' which segregates labour by 'privileged senior workers and their dispensable juniors' (Ibid). It also confirms his argument that since particularly junior faculty members are disposable due to the contract bases, they have to tolerate every mistreatment including bullying to maintain their job.

Limited Resources

One of the key challenges confronting respondents is the ubiquitous challenge of limited resources in the universities. Whilst the lack of resources in African universities abound in literature (e.g., Mohamedbhai, 2013; Materu, 2013), it has been argued that neoliberal university managers could deliberately limit access resources which could enhance work of faculty including time, money and space (Keashly and Neuman, 2010). From my own and respondents' experiences, in the context of limited resources, it is very difficult and at times almost impossible to satisfy all the demands and expectations on faculty including satisfying all the performance criteria for a contract to be renewed within a stipulated time. This is expressed by some of the responses below:

> I think the three years is good but if people can publish within the three years then we should put in place measures so that the institution does not lose the people. Some of the people are new in the academia so

they have to learn. And I do not think people will be able to learn to know all the tactics when it comes to writing and all that because it takes time. So you have to make sure that all the resources are available for the person to perform (Young academic).

And if they could do away with... someone has spent about six years here and you are just telling the person to just go meanwhile, you did not give the person enough resources to add value to himself then it becomes problematic (Young academic).

...there should be resources and there should be avenues to add value to yourself. For instance many universities are telling students to publish. Meanwhile if... (Mentions a name) needs data now there is no data stream. (Institution) does not subscribe to data stream. He has to link up with his colleagues in his formal university. So what about people who are here and they have not even crossed the border before...We are not well resourced (Young academic).

Now although it is very important that the contract is in place, it is good for people to perform, however, we should put in place, measures to help people to progress because if you are coming up with a contract base and you recruit someone for three years and after three years you say if you do not perform, the person is leaving and I know most people they are not able to perform in terms of publication and the people leave especially the younger ones because they do not have mentoring and all that (Young academic).

So you spend more time in recruiting people so you also have to make sure that that you retain them. Now how do you retain them? Because you spend a lot of money recruiting people, yes make sure that you put in place...so mentoring is good (Young academic).

Publication is good but if within the three years you have more people going out then it means that you have come to square one. The organisation is losing good people. So if you come and you do not have anyone to take you through or to help you it becomes very difficult (Young academic).

Impact on Young Academics

These neoliberal manifestation have varied impacts on teaching and learning outcomes, students' experiences and expectations, as well as faculty experiences. In this section, I will focus on faculty experiences. The varied demands, segregation, hierarchal decision making and competitive atmosphere have created varied negative impact on faculty, particularly in relation to their emotions. Below I discuss some few of them:

Fear and Suspicion

Responses from participants revealed great fear and suspicion. These emotions were explicitly expressed particularly in relation to the contract system. As one participant explained:

> Sometimes I feel scared because for me I always have to make sure I plan my time well. I am studying and I am working at the same time and I always make sure there is a balance because if I don't do well in the PHD programme then no one is going to say that I was working whilst on the programme. So the fear is always there. Even apart from studying and working, I always have to make sure that I meet the performance criteria because I am being assessed based on research, community work and publication. I am doing all these things just to make sure that when the three years is due, I will be able to renew my contract.

Where respondents thought they will be able to meet the performance criteria they were unsure of whether they will still be retained as they thought the renewal of contracts is not really based on merits but by who is favoured by management.

As explained by another respondent:

> Then when it comes to the six years, getting to the terminal point of that contract then comes the biggest problem. The question is are you out or in? How do you solve the problem of out or in... which is dependent on somebody in the society whether your dean wants to retain you or he does not want to retain you. So it depends on whether you are in the good

books of your dean or bad books of your Dean. So if someone is to determine your life in this way, how do you do it? If you go to court and your life depends on the judge's judgment on whether he likes you or dislikes you...? (Young academic)

...and those who are going to sit down on it, you know they have some peculiar type of people with certain qualifications who must decide on what to do, whether to give or not to give it to you... and they are professors or people that they have pulled to their group and so your fate is decided by those at the top and you do not know what it is going to be... So if you ask me what I think about it what do I do because I have to wait for them to decide on whether or not they are giving you... (Young academic)

Instability and Risk

These fear and suspicions create a sense of instability. Another respondent explained:

The contract, we have the three year and six year contract. So if you are giving these short contracts it has its own risks, for example, if a person is giving that short contract and the person is supposed to seek for promotion otherwise s/he will be kicked out of the university, it becomes worrisome. Because then you are not stable, you are not stable. You think you have a threat that you need to overcome. There is a blockage. Now how do you overcomes these blockades when you have a short time to think...in three years, they are going to sack me so what do I do so you are under desperation and you begin to act in different ways.

Competition and Individuality

Respondents indicated that such practices have created a competitive environment. The competition, excessive demands, ego building and segregation have led to individualism as each individual wishes to be recognized and somehow appreciated. As one respondent explained:

...because it is based on merit, then there is a lot of competition which I think is not the best... so when there is competition then the elderly people are not willing to help the younger one because you might think that if I help the person then the person might probably overtake me so I think that is one issue although merit base is good but it brings about a lot of competition which I think it is not the best because when you bring competition then people are not prepared to help others (Young academic).

Others also explained that individuals hide projects for funding and other activities they are engaged in from colleagues in order to get ahead of others. All these lead to toxic and unhealthy environment which affect both individual and organizational output. However, in the context of neoliberalism such individualism is unfortunately perceived as freedom (Davies & Bansel, 2007, 249)

Sense of Ambivalence

The responses from participants portrayed their sense of ambivalence. Ambivalence involves a simultaneous experience of positive and negative emotional or cognitive orientations towards a person, situation, object, task, or goal (Rothman, et al. n.d. 2). It was common to see the majority of respondents expressing much concern and worry about the contract systems, level of competition and segregation, among others and then just the next moment espouse these same ideologies. For instance concerning the contract system and faculty assessment the majority of the same individuals who expressed worry had these to say:

> So if you are given a long term contract, and I am looking at the contract in the sense that.... it is good. For instance if you give me tenure whether I progress or I add value to myself I will still be here. It does not help the institution. Because imagine I came here and there was not a little pressure on me to do something, I will have been sitting same. So that is the positive side of it, if you are given a long term contract (Young academic)

Concerning the assessment a participant who had earlier expressed worry had this to say:

I think it is good because we are in a global world and…if you want to be competitive then you have to make sure that quality is all that we are talking about.

And yet another one:

There should be competition…because at the end of the day, we are talking about value. The era we find ourselves it is all about quality (Young academic)

I think that the merit base is better and that is what the neoliberalism is about unlike previously when we were looking at seniority based approach so depending on how long you have been in the inst. So what I will say is that it has its own advantages and disadvantages here.

It could be seen from the responses that there were some levels of ambiguity, contradictions and uncertainties. The same people who express various challenges could be seen now supporting the concept. Though a sense of ambivalence have some benefits, the wider literature emphasise major disadvantages including discomfort, internal conflicts, reduced ability to decide, resistance to change, one-sided, narrow thinking and bias, and paralysis (van Harreveld, et al. 2015, Rothman, et al. n.d.).

Deterioration

These negative could have serious effect on the mental health of faculty. One participant explained:

It affects your emotional being, the psychological effects. Sometimes you can deteriorate. Some can even start talking whilst they are not discussing with anybody. The genesis of madness…

We all have to ask ourselves when we came here and it is good that we are talking with people who came here with MPhil or Msc. It takes time to understand this whole issue about publication. So if I am given a three year contract, where do I… you see you will be torn between trying to… establish yourself. We are in an institution where first and foremost teaching should become your priority. That is why you are here so that your students will understand you but before you could say jack, the three years will be up and you may be kicked out.

Many writers have expressed concern about how sustained focus on economic efficiency, audit, performability and intensifying competition have created a lot of a anxiety and mental ill health in academics (Huijbens and Larsen, 2016). Whilst the contexts of these writers may be different, the responses indicate these effects are very relevant to the context of Ghana.

Total Output and Learning Outcome

Such negative emotions generate tensions which impact negatively on teaching, learning outcomes and management of the institutions. For instance, as academics perceive themselves as unimportant and segregated against, they may decide to keep quite on matters affecting the institution. In this case, universities are deprived of the intellectual engagement, knowledge, skills and abilities of faculty. It affects team work, dedication and love for the work. Such attitudes are illustrated from responses of participants as indicated below:

> I think that brings a lot of tension because sometimes people do not want to talk. They feel okay I am not there yet so let me keep quiet, and even if I contribute they might not take not my information I am bringing on board along (Young academic).

> I am an HR person and I believe that as Human beings, we all assist the organization (Young academic).

> Sometimes it doesn't give you that free will to… because if you look at the future you do not have future with the work you are doing. So then where is the love for the work (Young academic)?

> In lieu of their personal interest and that really subjects other members of the community to risk which makes them feel un-belonged and therefore end up giving their minimum best. So the capitalism idea

could be pursued to the highest yet you wouldn't get the result you want because other subordinates do not fully feel as part of the system do not feel to be shareholders of the system and therefore will do their…So certain issues like contracts as you have said, must be looked at very well (Young academic).

These responses indicate that institution may suffer irrespective of the level of surveillance and the number of checks, without the inner motivation, commitment and love of the individual.

I will not say neoliberal approaches are without any benefits. There have been arguments that neoliberalism could have varied opportunities (e.g., Morley; 2003). For instance, 'each new mode of regulation creates new possibilities' (Hey and Bradford 2004, 693). The pressures of massification and managerialism have compelled universities to be more creative, initiative and improve infrastructure. Neoliberalism could also present real opportunities to eliminate oppressive practices (Becher and Trowler 2001, 18). In the institutions, there are certain infrastructural and other developmental changes that have occurred which could be perceived mainly as resulting from neoliberal ideas. As one thinks about these benefits, one cannot also ignore the political, economic, cultural and psychological tensions underlying these changes (Harris 2011; Torres, 2002).

It could be inferred from the responses that neoliberal ideologies have serious negative consequences particularly, on young academics who are now creating their identities in the career. Whilst it may affect their career, it also has implications on their mental health. It is important that the universities adopt pragmatic policies and practices that will not worsen the tensions in the universities and the larger society.

RECOMMENDATIONS

Considering the extent of neoliberal agendas in universities, it is imperative that universities adopt strategies to mitigate effects on particularly young academics to enhance institutional desired goals. The following interventions are suggested to enhance student experiences in the universities and to fulfil their goals in life.

Creating Awareness of the Concept of Neoliberalism and Its Impact on Academics

It is important that universities create awareness and resist neoliberal ideologies as dominant ideologies governing universities. Neoliberalism should not be seen as a non-replaceable concept neither should its influences be taken for granted. There should be much research into the impact of neoliberalism on higher educational institutions. Efforts should be made to have alternative strategies to achieve the desired goals of the universities both nationally and internationally.

Mentoring

With the changing context of higher education and its performativity, it is important to emphasise formal mentoring processes to enhance retention of faculty, their career development and their physical and emotional well-being. These will enhance their general output of institutions (e.g., Carmel and Paul 2015).

The process of mentoring should be more than advising. Mentors should be identified who will devout time, energy and even emotions. The competitive and demanding landscape in Higher Education have made it more difficult for experienced academics to invest in and support their professorial and personal development of junior academics. However, the mentoring process has immense benefits including encouraging mentors to feel appreciated by organisation as they feel their knowledge and experience are valued by their peers and managers. Mentees also realise that the institution is prepared to invest in their future. It promotes enthusiasm, raise self-esteem and self-confidence of both mentors and mentees and provides a safety net for career-related frustrations (Carmel and Paul 2015). Ultimately, junior academics will develop maturity, confidence, and autonomy and become more reflective about learning experiences (Carmel and Paul 2015).

Promoting African Journals

There is the need for universities to promote African journals. African journals have been marginalized in university presses and world data base (e.g., Murray and Clobridge, 2014). Unfortunately, this marginalization is being perpetuated by African universities which continue to perceive African journals as inferior to Western journals. Firstly, it appears difficult for particularly early career African scholars to publish in many of the Western journals and if one is lucky for a paper to be accepted, it could take a longer time for it to be published. Whilst recognizing and appreciating African journals would help particularly junior academics to maintain and progress in their career it will also enhance positioning of African journals internationally.

Many writers have confirmed the criticality and the need for African scholars and publishers to emphasise African journal to improve access, visibility and impact (e.g., Ezema, 2010; Murray and Clobridge, 2014, Rosenberg, 2002).

Provision of Resources

As indicated earlier, literature is bourgeoned with financial constraints of African universities. (e.g., Materu, 2007). Whilst these constraint are appreciated, it is still essential, considering the expectations and demands on faculty, that management make explicit efforts to ensure resources including time and space to enhance the personal and professional development of particularly junior academics. The universities must strive to position themselves internationally to be able to attract funding and also for individuals from these institutions to attract funding. In spite of the limited resources, power imbalance, limitations and hostility, the individual is blamed as lazy, incompetent which affects the self-worth of academics and their own identities. For instance, mostly, as respondents attested, should they fail to be promotable at the end of their contract year, they will be held responsible and not the limitations they are confronted with.

Promotion of a Sense of Belonging

Mainly, to compel faculty to fulfill all demands, varied checks and surveillance strategies have been implemented but it is significant to reiterate that without a sense of belonging and inner commitment from individuals, it will be difficult for the institutions to achieve their desired goals. Management should deemphasize segregation and discriminations. Efforts should be made to let all individual feel they have something to offer to his or her institution. Again, efforts should be made to reduce the high sense of ambivalence of staff as this result in varied negative emotions.

CONCLUSION

Neoliberalism has gradually become endemic in higher educational institutions in Ghana. Its ideologies have impacted on varied aspects of the institutions including infrastructural development, curriculum development, expectations and demands of academics, and restructuring of departments. Whilst there are some positive implications, the disadvantages appear overwhelming. More significantly is what has been argued as declaration of war on academics (Giroux, 2014). The majority of young academics, for instance, are confronted with many challenges including individualism, job insecurity and excessive stress. Inequalities and meritocracy have become the norm. These manifestations negatively impact on identities of academics and their performance (Archer, 2008; Naidoo and Jamieson, 2007, 269).

Few voices, however, seem to be challenging the takeover of the neoliberal agenda and little is being done to resist its ideologies at both the national and institutional levels. It is recommended for the institutions to embark on strategies to create awareness of these neoliberal ideologies and their influences and undertake research to identify ways to mitigate their effects. Universities should rethink about their unflinching adoption and commitment to neoliebeal ideologies and to explore alternative strategies to satisfy their national and international needs. It is also critical for universties to identify optimum conditions to enhance personal and career development of faculty. This could be achieved through varied activities and policies including formal and informal mentorship programmes, provision of resources, promotion of local journals and participatory decision making.

REFERENCES

Archer, L. (2008). The new neoliberal subjects? Young/er academics' constructions of professional identity, *Journal of Education Policy*, 23:3, 265-285.

Ayelazuno, J. A. (2013). Neoliberalism and Growth without Development in Ghana: A Case for State-led Industrialization. *Journal of Asian and African Studies,* 49:1, 80-99.

Becher, T., and Trowler, P. (2001). *Academic tribes and territories* (2nd ed.). Buckingham: SRHE/Open Univ. Press.

BERA, (2004) *Revised Ethical Guidelines for Educational Research,* Available at: http://www.bera.ac.uk/files/2008/09/ethic1.pdf (accessed 13/02/2011).

Block, D. (2018). Some thoughts on education and the discourse of global neoliberalism, *Language and Intercultural Communication,* 18:5, 576-584, doi: 10.1080/14708477.2018.1501851.

Boafo-Arthur, K., (ed.) (2007) *Ghana, One Decade of the Liberal State*, Dakar: Codesria Books; Pretoria: In association with Unisa Press; Accra: EPP Book Services; London-New York: Zed Books.

Cannella, G. S., & Koro-Ljungberg, M. (2017). Neoliberalism in higher education: Can we understand? Can we resist and survive? Can we become without neoliberalism? *Cultural Studies Critical Methodologies*, 17:3, 155–162.

Collins, P. (2017). Where have all the flowers gone? In S. Riddle, M. K. Harmes, & P. A. Danaher (Eds.), *Producing pleasure in the contemporary university. Bold visions in educational research*, 59. Rotterdam: Sense Publishers.

Creswell, J. W. (2007). *Qualitative inquiry & research design: Choosing among five approaches*. Thousand Oaks, CA: Sage Publications, Inc.

Currie, J., B. Thiele, and P. Harris, (2002) *Gendered Universities in Globalised Economies: Power, careers and sacrifices,* Lanham, MD: Lexington Books.

Dardot, P., & Laval, C. (2013). *The new way of the world: On a neoliberal society*. London: Verso.

Davies, B. & Bansel, P. (2007). Governmentality and academic work: shaping the hearts and minds of academic workers. *Journal of Curriculum Theorizing* July 23:2, 9-26.

Desjardins, R., (2013) 'Considerations of the Impact of Neoliberalism and Alternative Regimes on Learning and its Outcome: An empirical example based on the level and distribution of adult learning', *International Studies in Sociology of Education*, 23:3, 102-203.

DeSouza, E. R. (2011). Frequency rates and correlates of contrapower harassment in higher education. *Journal of Interpersonal Violence,* 26:1, 158–188.

Donkor, D. A. (2016). *Spiders of the Market: Ghanaian Trickster Performance in a Web of Neoliberalism*. African Expressive Cultures: Indiana University Press.

Ehrich LC, Hansford B and Tennent L (2004) Formal mentoring programs in education and other professions: A review of the literature. *Educational Administration Quarterly* 40:4, 518–540.

Ezema, I. J. (2010). Trends in electronic journal publishing in Africa: An analysis of African Journal Online (AJOL). *Webology* 7(1).

Fourcode, M. and K. Healy, (2007) Moral views of market society, *The Annual Review of Sociology*, Available at: http://soc.annualreviews.org.

Girdwood, A., (1999) *Tertiary Education Policy in Ghana: An assessment, 1988- 1998,* Education, the World Bank, Available at:http://chet.org.za/manual/media/files/chet_hernana_docs/Ghana.

Giroux, H. A (2014). Neoliberalism, Democracy and the University as a Public Sphere An interview by Victoria Harper. *Policy Futures in Education,* 12:8, 1078-1083.

Given, L. M. 2008. *The Sage Encyclopaedia of Qualitative Research Methods.* Thousand Oaks: Sage Publication Inc.

Government White Paper on the Report of the Education (2007) *Reform Review Committee,* Accra.

Gyamera G. O and Burke, P. J. (2017): Neoliberalism and curriculum in higher education: a post-colonial analyses, *Teaching in Higher Education,* doi:10.1080/13562517.2017.1414782.

Gyamera, G. O. (2015) The internationalisation agenda: a critical examination of internationalisation strategies in public universities in Ghana. *International Studies in Sociology of Education*, 25:2, 112-131, doi: 10.1080/09620214.2015.1034290.

Gyamera, G. O. (2018): The Internationalisation Agenda: a critical look at the conceptualisation and rationalisation of internationalisation in public universities in Ghana, Compare: *A Journal of Comparative and International Education*, doi: 10.1080/03057925.2018.1474729.

Harris, S., (2011) *University in Translation: Internationalising higher education.* Britain: Continuum International Publishing Group.

Harvey, D., (2005) *A Brief History of Neoliberalism,* Oxford University Press.

Hey, V. and Bradford, S. (2004). The return of the repressed? The gender politics of emergent forms of professionalism in education. *Journal of Education Policy* 19:6, 691–713.

Jones, G., (2013) 'Afterword: Rates of Exchange: Neoliberalism and the value of higher education', *International Studies in Sociology of Education,* 23:3, 273-280.

Keashly, L., and Neuman, J. H. (2010). Faculty Experiences with bullying in higher education. *Administrative Theory & Praxis,* 32:1, 48–70.

Kent L. G. and Arthur, A. N. (2017) Improving Academic Mentoring Relationships and Environments. *Acoustical Society of America.* 13:3.

Kotz, D. 2015. *The rise and fall of neoliberal capitalism.* Cambridge MA: Harvard University Press.

Materu. P. (2007). Higher Education Quality Assurance in Sub-Saharan Africa: Status, Challenges, Opportunities, and Promising Practices. *Africa Region Human Development Department World Bank working paper no. 124.*

Mohamedbhai, G. (2013). Towards an African higher education and research space (AHERS). *A Summary Report. Working Group on Higher Education (WGHE).* Association for the development of education in African dialogue on education for leadership change. Working group on higher education (WEHE).

Morley, L. 2003. *Quality and power in Higher Education.* Maidenhead: Open University Press.

Munene, I. I., (2008) Privatising the Public: Marketization as a strategy in public University transformation, *Research in Post- Compulsory Education,* 13:1, 1-17.

Murray, S. and Clobridge, A. (2014). The Current State of Scholarly Journal Publishing in Africa: Findings & Analysis. *African Journal Online.* Retrieved from: https://www.ajol.info/public/Scholarly-Journal-Publishing-in-Africa-Report-Final-v04c.pdf

Naidoo, R, and I., Jamieson, (2007) Knowledge in the Marketplace: The global commodification of teaching and learning in higher education, in Ninnes, P., and M. Hellstein (eds.) *Internationalizing Higher Education,* Netherlands: Springer.

Norris, M. A. (2019). Neoliberalism's demons, *Political Theology,* doi: 10.1080/1462317X.2019.1583788.

Oleksiyenko, A. (2018) Zones of alienation in global higher education: corporate abuse and leadership failures, *Tertiary Education and Management,* 24:3, 193-205, doi: 10.1080/13583883.2018.1439095.

Omtzist, D., (2008) in Agyeman Duah, I (ed.) An economic history of Ghana: Reflections on a half- century of challenges and progress (eds) UK: Ayebia Clarke publishing limited Pololi L and Knight S (2005) Mentoring faculty in academic medicine: A new paradigm? *Journal of General Internal Medicine* 20:9, 866–870.

Roofe G. Carmel Miller W. Paul (2015). Mentoring and coaching in academia: Reflections on a mentoring/coaching relationship. *Policy Futures in Education* 13:4, 479–491.

Rosenberg, D. (2002) African Journals Online: improving awareness and access. *Learned Publishing* 15, 51–57.

Rothman, N. B., Pratt M. G., Rees, L, Vogus, T. J. (2016). Understanding The Dual Nature of Ambivalence: Why and When Ambivalence Leads to Good and Bad Outcomes. *Academy of Management Annals,* 11:1.

Shakouri N. (2014). Qualitative Research: Incredulity toward Metanarrativeness. *Journal of Education and Human Development,* 3:2, 671-680.

Tonah, S., (2009) The Unending Cycle of Education Reform in Ghana, *JERA/RARE* 1, pp. 45-52.

Torres, C. A., (2011) Public Universities and the Neoliberal Common Sense: seven iconoclastic theses, *International studies in sociology of education* 21:3.

Torres, C. A., and G. Jones, (2013) Neoliberal Common Sense in Education: Part two. *International Studies in Sociology of Education,* 23:3, 179-181.

van Harreveld, F., Nohlen, H. U. and Schneider, I. K. (2015). *The ABC of Ambivalence: Affective, Behavioral, and Cognitive Consequences of Attitudinal Conflict Advances in Experimental Social Psychology.* Elsevier Inc.

Windle, J. (2019) Neoliberalism, imperialism and conservatism: tangled logics of educational inequality in the global South. *Discourse: Studies in the Cultural Politics of Education*, 40:2, 191-202.

In: Neoliberalism
Editor: Travis Graham
ISBN: 978-1-53616-014-7
© 2019 Nova Science Publishers, Inc.

Chapter 3

AUTOCRACY VS. NEOLIBERALISM: A UKRAINIAN TEST CASE

*Žilvinas Svigaris**, *MD*
Faculty of Phillosophy, Vilnius University, Vilnius, Lithuania

ABSTRACT

One more country decided to take a risk and see what it means to become liberal and democratic. Although liberal democracy is often considered as the best form of human government, currently it is facing a so-called neoliberal crisis that has brought unexpected and disruptive results of uneven sharing of power and wealth in society. Capital concentration in natural oligopolies and corporate control become almost unresolvable problems facing modern economies. This paper will explore here the possibilities of transitioning from isolated monoliths of oligopolies into an ecosystem of a modular economy that is based on small or medium, competitive, community friendly and flexible enterprises. This trend stimulates the creation of a self-driven society that does not depend exclusively on the local economic situation anymore but can benefit from globally accessible opportunities. Ukraine is right at the core of the geostrategic concerns and not only because of the geopolitical

---

* Corresponding Author's E-mail: zilvinas.svigaris@fsf.vu.lt.

location of the country but mainly because it raises questions that are relevant to all liberal democracies in the world that are troubled by after-effects of neoliberal policies. Although there is still a high risk that Ukraine might end up going off the rails into the systemic corruption again[1], there is also hope of seeing the transformation of the current neoliberal system into a new self-driven society able to solve problems of safety and employment in the country. However, let us start with events that took place in Ukraine almost four years ago, from the Revolution of Dignity.

Keywords: Ukraine, neoliberalism, revolution of dignity, democracy, self-driven society.

INTRODUCTION

Before the so-called Revolution of Dignity, Ukraine had almost 300 years of lasting close relations with Russia, but not as most other nations, which were never really happy to struggle under Moscow's dictatorship. Ukraine was the most critical partner in all of Moscow's affairs, and up until the last moment, many of the most essential, vital and strategic Russian manufacturing resources were located in Ukraine. Therefore, the split has been much more painful than expected. But, why split? Four years ago, Ukraine decided to go the Eurocentric way. It is interesting that there were no leaders who organized the revolution; it happened almost spontaneously. The Ukrainian people suddenly and unexpectedly understood that they are different from their neighboring Russians. The difference was in the character of the individuals, in the understanding that they can stand for themselves, not only as Ukrainians fighting for political change but also as individuals rediscovering their dignity. Although the memory of being poor and insecure is still here, the struggle for human dignity is changing the political and economic environment in this significant region. In other words, the Ukrainian revolution is based not only on economic or political reasons; this revolution is significant because

---

[1] Ukraine is ranked 131 out of 176 countries in Transparency International's Corruption Perception Index in 2017.

of the recognition of the Ukrainian nation as a community of self-driven individuals able to thrive in the contemporary world. I remember well the struggle for becoming dignified citizens of our own country that led the Lithuanian Singing revolution against the Soviet Union almost 30 years ago. Ukrainians have shown once more that militarized despotic power has a decreasing impact on the historical events in the world and cannot stop the voice of the people if they have made their decision for a transformation of the country.

Ukraine has started remarkably intensive transformation and reconstruction of the country on all levels. The intensity of renovation of the country's infrastructure is so immense that it seems there was no precedent for such vast positive changes in the past. The opportunity for reform of education, economic, political and other systems has been long awaited since the collapse of the Soviet Union. Until the revolt started at the Maidan, Ukraine had been managed by the central autocratic puppet government that depended on directions coming from Moscow. Those directions were premised on the idea that the real needs of a person are much simpler than they are often thought to be, and people feel poverty only when they discover that their neighbor is living better. Thus, the autocratic, dictatorial regime cynically uses this and keeps the population trapped inside the borders of the country. Even today, only a small percentage of people in Russian people can afford to get an international passport allowing them to leave the country. Also, heavy censorship of the Internet and proliferation of propaganda create apocalyptic stories about supposed Western decadence by turning the autocrat into the image of a savior, master of the people and the nation. Exploitation of such a despotic regime kept Ukraine in backwardness, corruption and kleptocracy. However, the population of the country understood that this could not go on any further and that all their difficulties were surmountable. They understood that their problems arose because of bad human decisions but human decisions could be changed if the Ukrainian people fought for their dignity. Therefore, this is not nationalism against Russians, as sometimes advocated in the media. This point is worth exploring in more detail.

The *nationalism* that is propagated from above has to be separated here from the individual recognition of *national dignity* that is coming from *below*. Nationalism is a political tool that is intended to replace real *national identity* and dignity of the individual with a political attitude that is aggressive, chauvinistic and offensive to other nations or countries. Autocratic politics use *nationalism* as a propaganda tool to come to power and to use one community of people against the others. Viktor Orbán in Hungary, Vladimir Putin in Russia, Recep Tayyip Erdoğan in Turkey, Marine Le Pen in France and many other populist leaders use the *nationalism* argument to manipulate feelings of the people and to use them as a political tool. *Nationalism*, in the end, makes society limited and week. It is almost opposite to true *national dignity*. It is entirely different in Ukraine's case. *National dignity* and independence in Ukraine have grown from the bottom, from the grassroots, from a united initiative of an active people of the country, without a clearly defined leader. National identity is naturally fermenting from the bottom upwards; it should be acknowledged freely and without obfuscations. This is precisely what the Ukrainian people have understood. Ukrainians recreated their nation, not by becoming *nationalistic* in the narrow sense of this word, but by reclaiming their vivid, modest and laborious national character, together with deep national and ethnic roots in language, customs, national cuisine and their famous attire[2]. At the same time, it is worth noting that modernization processes transform not only the political and economic systems of the country but also traditional values and national identity. Samuel Huntington emphasizes that many countries strive to import just the modernization and protect themselves from westernization[3]. This is not the case with Ukraine because it is striving to become part of Western Europe, though not through assimilation or losing their *national dignity* in westernization processes, but rather by changing their political-economic structure and benefiting from liberal democratic reforms.

---

[2] Author of the paper has just returned from visiting Kyiv and other Ukraine cities where many Ukrainians have been proudly wearing their astonishing and famous national attire.
[3] Huntington 1996, 72.

LIBERAL DEMOCRACY

Why liberal democracy? Everybody understands that this political system does not guarantee that all groups of people in the country will reach their targets. But strongman politics are even worse; they go much further without satisfying any interests except one – that of the autocrat. The primary target of the autocrat is to use the power to protect his legitimacy, and he cannot risk sharing the power with any competitor. Despite the fact that it is still extremely difficult to solve all problems, liberal democracy at least offers the possibility of a peaceful change from authority to representation. Therefore, liberal democracy gives hope that the power of the state in Ukraine will be shared and democratic procedures will open possibilities for positive reforms. Furthermore, this is the most persuasive argument that positioned Ukraine on the way towards liberal democracy. The second argument is an extremely high correlation between stable liberal democracies and the highest levels of economic, scientific, educational, legal development and prosperity in the world. Democratic countries like those in Western Europe, North America and Japan that are advanced technologically are liberal democracies. While, according to Francis Fukuyama, who claims that liberal democracy may signal the end point of humanity's sociocultural evolution and become the final and the best form of human government, it seems that it is not enough just to declare liberal democracy in order to improve the country's wealth and safety. Citizens of the country should develop a stable state, the rule of law and most importantly – accountability. In other words, the government has to be accountable to independent citizens. The prosperity of the country will not grow by itself; citizens have to create and maintain this growth. Without active participation of citizens, even liberal democracy can become problematic.

When we are talking about liberal democracies, there is an increasing number of claims[4] and recognition that almost all liberal democracies in the contemporary world represent different forms of so-called

---

[4] Noam Chomsky, Thomas Ferguson, James Crotty, et.al..

neoliberalism. Neoliberalism is almost never clearly defined and has primarily become a term of condemnation employed by critics. Neoliberalism demands the elimination of government intervention in the domestic economy and abolition of barriers to free movement of goods and capital across national boundaries and suggests free market principles[5]. Neoliberal enthusiasts promised that this new laissez-faire era would dramatically improve economic performance in both developed and developing countries. Unfortunately, these promises have not been kept.[6] Neoliberalism has brought unexpected and disruptive results, which are summarized by the famous saying that the economy is doing fine, but the people are not. There are no exceptions to the rule that neoliberalism generates rising inequality everywhere.[7] Historian Daniel Stedman Jones rightly notes that the term neoliberalism has become a catch-all expression for the horrors associated with globalization and recurring financial crises.[8] It is widely recognized that corporations are prospering at the expense of the broader community. Private capital accumulation has been concentrated in natural oligopolies, which have also been the sites of the implementation, if not always the invention, of the most productive economic innovations.[9]

Disproportions and deformations of communities brought by neoliberalism threaten to disrupt the very fundaments of liberal democracy because the growth of economy and power of a country do not carry wealth and security for citizens of that country. In other words, neoliberal policies mostly are created and maintained by lobbyists who represent very concrete interests of specific groups of people. Many programs are created to solve the interests of the minority at the expense of the majority of society. This continues to increase the economic and political gap between the business elite and the majority of the citizenry. So-called oligarchs try to reach personal targets by using the politics of the country. Therefore, those who have the most significant impact on political and economic

---

[5] Kotz 1998, 2.
[6] Crotty 2000, 1.
[7] Crotty & Kang-Kook 2002, 9.
[8] Stedman 2012, 15.
[9] Crotty 2000, 18.

reforms at the same time get the most substantial profit from them; they are mostly hiding under the umbrella of financial institutions which have increased significantly during neoliberal reforms.[10] Without social accountability, private or despotic powers have no limitations for their concentrations. The fundamental doctrine of neoliberalism was well expressed by Adam Smith: the vile maxim of the masters of mankind, all for ourselves and nothing for other people. If the masters are given free rein, then we should expect a social and economic disaster. Most corporate enterprises are focused on value creation, narrowly optimizing short-term financial performance and disregarding the broader influences that determine longer-term benefits for society, including all initiatives to maintain improvement of labor conditions.

On the other hand, caring about long-term benefits to society is also an indirect expense of enterprise. Therefore, the price of a service or a product should contain the additive cost that is used to improve labor conditions. However, this additional cost often makes the product not competitive in the market where a price war dominates. Hence, it is increasingly difficult to induce long-lived profitable investment in the unprofitable and uncertain environment that destructive competition generates.[11] More than that, to the surprise of a short-sighted enthusiast of Western neoliberal politics, the growth of globalization of markets resulted in a growth of competition. Eastern "miracles" brought especially fierce competition in almost all possible spheres that ended with significant economic and social tensions. Neoliberalism changed not only prices of products. It is worth noting that after rejecting the tradition of improvement of labor conditions, neoliberalism brought sharp undercuts of social commitments. Accompanied by growth of monstrous and predatory financial institutions that worried only about their survival in the competitive market, it has brought the crisis of the social sector. Instead of working for the people and evenly sharing the resources, corporate institutions care about a concentration of those resources and investments into corporate power. Powerful economic elites, especially in the US, firstly pursue survival in

---

[10] Chomsky 2017, 48:12.
[11] Crotty 2000, 18.

the market, rather than serving public interests. Hence, instead of bringing prosperity to countries, neoliberalism brought tensions, anger and fear followed by neglect of the population and dignity of citizens of the country. James Crotty summarizes that neoliberal theory is deeply flawed in all its forms; it is a misleading and dangerous guide for institution building and government economic policymaking.[12] In other words, global neoliberalism is moving the world towards a disappointing and perhaps disastrous economic future.

POST-SOVIET REFORMS

After the 1991 Soviet bloc collapse, Ukraine's connection with Russia remained very close in almost all spheres. Both countries decided to try an experiment of neoliberalism and showed once more what happens if the full conditions of a free market utopia are actually fulfilled. As analyses demonstrated, nowhere was the neoliberal mission more successful in destroying social and economic trends than in Russia, where President Boris Yeltsin took the simplistic neoliberal theory seriously and did his best to follow the neoliberal prescription to the letter. The result of the neoliberal experiment in Russia was economic devastation on a scale unseen anywhere else during peacetime after the Second World War. In just a few years, according to official statistics, Russia's GDP and its investment in new plants and equipment dropped drastically.[13] The same happened in Ukraine. Shock treatment in the form of free-market policies recommended by American advisers wiped out the economies of Russia and Ukraine and created a corrupt, semi-criminal, ex-communist oligarch system merged with a clan of autocratic political bureaucracy. The unleashing of oligarchs[14] in Ukraine downgraded the population to a level of almost unimaginable poverty. Most of the pensioners receive pensions

---

[12] Crotty 2000, 29.
[13] Kotz 1998, 4.
[14] The term "oligarch" denotes a post-Soviet industrial and/or financial magnate who "controls sufficient resources to influence national politics" (Guriev & Rachinsky 2005, 131).

of 42€[15] which limit the chances of survival unless they grow their own fruits and vegetables in small backyard plots[16]. In other words, neoliberal reforms to Post-Soviet Russia and Ukraine were extremely destructive. They pushed the countries into a much broader crisis than when they were in the isolated Soviet system. Those reforms escalated the number of deaths that have resulted from increases in alcoholism, suicide and murder, infectious diseases, and stress-related ailments. Just like other countries which dared to venture into the neoliberal experiment, Russia and Ukraine are facing consequences of the sharp inequality between wealthy and poor, with incredibly devastating effects. Therefore, the Revolution of Dignity is not only a political revolt against despotic autocrats, it is not only the revelation of national dignity, but it is also the uprising of the Ukrainian population against poverty. Neoliberal reforms have destroyed the conditions required for a productive, symbiotic relationship between the government and the economy, between the state and the market and between micro- and macroeconomic activities.[17]

Restoring normal conditions of safe living and recreation of the country starts from normalization of relations between government and the society. We should keep in mind that the success or failure of liberal democratic reforms in Ukraine is closely connected with aspects of everyday life such as safety, employment, access to healthcare, education and social spending. This critical point is worth exploring in depth. The intensive transformations of Ukraine were started as a revolt by the people of the country, who showed that they have enough character to protect their dignity. However, weaknesses of the country, especially safety and poverty, cannot be solved merely by addressing the dignity. Restoring normal conditions of living and safety in the country can be reached by re-creating education, political and economic foundations. It is important to emphasize that optimistic expectations for revitalizing and reforming a democratic society in Ukraine should be built not on corrupt bureaucracy and oligopolies, but on the social principles that are centered on equality

---

[15] Rybak 2017.
[16] Kotz 1998, 4.
[17] Crotty 2000, 24.

and human dignity. The Ukrainian ambassador to Canada, Andriy Shevchenko, rightly notes that there is a danger such that after killing the dragon to become the dragon.[18] Although there is no doubt that political changes are rapid and irreversible, the situation is changing slowly. It is crucial to preserve the enthusiasm of society, looking for the possibilities to convert it to new progressive activities in science, politics, economy and other spheres. Nevertheless, even if citizens are united and have a good will, they often lack understanding of political and macroeconomic subtleties. There is no trust in any new system if it does not bring safety, chances to survival and earning a living. Hence, it is vitally important for the government to take care of improving conditions of people's livelihood, without waiting for a better economic situation. The government should provide opportunities for people to solve their problems by themselves from the very beginning. How can this be accomplished?

LOCAL COMMUNITIES

There are many projects in Ukraine planning investments that will be poured into mega industrial and agricultural projects, which strengthen the country's economy and use the potential of big corporations. However, the most important project and the most significant potential of any country is its people. It is critical to treat people as equal citizens, and although no country has reached perfection, some societies are doing much better than others. If the people see themselves ignored and suppressed, their hope for the future will decrease, and contempt for political and financial institutions will increase. Therefore, it is important to invest in the people of the country, especially those who begin to perceive themselves as able to become self-driven. It is very important to nurture those who can create working places instead of using them, those who can create a productive and positive environment not only for themselves but also for others. Even

---

[18] Fukuayma 2017.

a small percent of inspired and enthusiastic people can determine the welfare of a city or a region. The Ukrainians have already started to create communities which solve their local issues by themselves because people participate in decision making. Instead of an amorphous mass of individuals, active communities emerge that create visions of their future and implement them. Creating local communities is a major component of good societies[19]. This is especially true in Ukraine where new leaders strive to dismember corruptive schemes and are trying to change the situation. The country can solve problems faster thanks to those who are open-mindedly and actively engaged in transformation processes, who are motivated to change the living conditions. The role of such leaders and promoters of radical reforms is to say – "Look, it doesn't have to be like this." It is essential to support people who want to change the country for the better.[20]

There are already good initiatives towards the creation of a self-driven society in Ukraine. Let us look briefly at one of them which was created two years ago in Novopskov Luhansk Oblast. The newly formed community of Novopskov can use the budget of the region for their local needs.[21] Previously only a small portion of the budget was given to the people of this region, but now the community itself decides what the budget is used for. Two years ago, the community of this district decided to eliminate bureaucratic nomenclature that was disproportionally large, expensive and ineffective. Also, instead of sending taxes to Kyiv, they now use those funds for local needs. Local people in the village, which was treated as a province without any promises, have changed dramatically. Now citizens are exploring their new possibilities and find themselves in a place of opportunities. People there get more jobs and are motivated to improve their living environment. The head of the Novopskov community Vadim Hayev emphasizes that the number of active citizens increased because they understood that they were important for society, that they could influence the quality of life and security of their district, together

---

[19] Etzioni 2000, 15.
[20] Manson 2016.
[21] Ukraineworld 2016.

with their possibilities. Local people created projects and found ways to make their town more comfortable to live in. Financial independence and self-reliance of local regions is essential because thanks to the development of communications, logistics and other infrastructures, there is less and less difference where one is located. Activities of local communities significantly contribute to the even distribution of the decentralized development of the country and this is critically important in all post-Soviet countries. This experience of self-management of regions can be transferred further to other regions, to make people able to stabilize a living environment, ensure safety and create employment. Also, this approach of making communities self-managed should be expanded to other areas like education, politics, and economics.

CREATIVE STRAND

People around the world are looking for dignified, independent lives. There is a strong social tendency to become independent and self-sufficient citizens, requiring no favors from authorities or bureaucrats. They aim at creating employment instead of looking for available jobs on the market. This means that those who work also create working places, and also control enterprises. The creation and selling of something created is not the same as selling yourself. Being co-owner and co-creator means that workers care about their business as much as their personal well-being. New enterprises are often built not on forms of exploitation and payment for work, but on creativity and a proportional share of profit for workers. People of such self-driven teams and communities create an entirely different kind of society. A society of creators, discoverers and innovators that can provoke each other and come up with ideas that have not been possible to realize before. Even more, these same people at the same time are the society of consumers that are shaping the market, choosing trends, fashions and preferences of tomorrow. Neoliberalism, with one-sided opportunities for the benefit of the wealthy members is already competing with so-called post-Ford business models that are adopted mostly by small and medium-sized enterprises (SME).

Many significant enterprises often literally grow from small teams, consisting of a few members without substantial investments or support from the outside at the very beginning. A small group of people with a good idea and enough persistence can create a technological breakthrough. Their innovations can radically transform an entire sector of the economy. Such teams are creating globally recognized solutions in many areas of human activity that can spread around the world in seconds, which not only generate high profits but change the understanding of the living world. Because of their effectiveness, those solutions blow away old technologies, approaches, and dated forms of infrastructure, in an incredibly short time. Rejection of old methods is so rapid that even academic books and courses in many universities are often behind the real pace of technology. However, this is happening naturally because some developers grow faster than others. Changing the leading technological preferences in the world often are made by the creativity of small or medium-sized teams of developers that can quickly attract attention and funds. It is worth mentioning that it is not an accident that SME's are the backbone of the EU economy. They do not only dominate but make up more than 99% of all enterprises. The tendency of small teams in the EU is also growing because of full automatization of production. There is a constant reduction in the number of employees doing manual operations and outsourcing those operations to suppliers in lower-wage locations. Employees in the EU and the US are increasingly doing work on marketing and innovation areas, building infrastructure, testing systems, giving lectures or facilitating retrospectives. Very often, more than half of an enterprise in one way or another involved in R&D processes. Modern industry is already following the idea that all manual operations should be automated. Economic growth is becoming more and more synonymous with inventions of new approaches, products, and services that are quickly transforming activity models in almost all spheres and quickly spreading around the world.

Globalization

Even small enterprises can act globally. The continuing decrease in transportation and communication costs has resulted in the realization of global economies on scales greater than were hardly possible even a few generations ago. A new generation of creators does not need to be located in one place anymore. Conferences and meetings are conducted on the internet more and more. Industry does not need to be in urbanized areas; it moves not only away from big cities, but also to different countries or continents. New forms of division of labor and social mobilization are becoming incredibly flexible, and team members geographically located in the most distant parts of the world can develop projects together, side-by-side. The new economic era's principal players are not only large corporations but even more small and medium-sized enterprises that can efficiently generate innovative ideas. Each enterprise occupies a niche that becomes part of the much larger so-called division of labor and characterizes the global creation of new economic opportunities for other enterprises. Solving specific problems and reaching the global audience increases possibilities tremendously. Stagnant and limited mentality is not competitive in the worldwide market anymore and can survive only by schemes of corruption. Needless to say, any closed-door politics are determined in the short run to be overrun by open-minded and creative approaches. Isolated corporations that will not become modular and flexible will not be competitive soon. Hence, new possibilities of global markets, which have been opened to Ukraine, together with vast opportunities, also bring intense competition.

We should emphasize, that global markets are extremely tight and demand a great deal from those who are entering them. The high level of automation and perfectly developed products make it almost impossible to enter most of the EU or US markets quickly. The competition in global manufacturing markets is so intense and fierce that a producer, without a unique product, has almost no chance of survival. Profit usually is just a small fraction of turnover, and if not regularly reinvested into innovations, can lead to bankruptcy. Development and innovation of the company is not just the target of a starting stage, but the key to survival in global markets. The global economy is not only the spread of activity through countries and continents, not only overcoming political and economic barriers; more importantly, the global economy means a new global vision that allows a meeting with the needs of every human being on the planet. Therefore, the creator needs to have in mind cultural diversity and the different mentality when creating products for worldwide global markets. Such teams of creators are multi-national not by chance, but on purpose. More than that, an aspect of multi-nationality becomes the real source of creativity. Differences among multi-cultural team members enable much wider possibilities of looking at the same world with different eyes. It is worth mentioning that such a creative working environment encourages enriching national identity and dignity because the creative process makes everybody equal and no one nation is "greater" than others; each member enriches the team with fruitful insights. Those team members are driven by a scientific, technology-based approach, enabling them to spread ideas on the global market through the Internet, media and bulk production. Technology becomes an essential instrument for the creation of wealth and safe society.

In the global environment, technologies are boosting so quickly that capital invested into new technology becomes irreversible in a shorter time than ever. The question of choosing the right technology to invest is critically important, mainly when investments in economies of scale entail a substantial risk of significant loss. Any investment should consider that profit rates can fall below average in a short-term and there will be no chance to exit except with capital loss or bankruptcy. It is evident that large enterprises hardly dependent on one specific product or service become risky in today's rapidly changing market for many reasons. There are many stories of leaders of the market that have been pushed out of leading positions in a short time. For instance, Kodak did not develop a digital camera and went bankrupt. Nokia was pushed out by smartphone producers, and the same is happening with petrol-driven cars and many other obsolete technologies. Even small changes in preferences of consumers can create or close specific markets; for instance, taxi companies that have built entire infrastructures over the years, are forced to close because of the more comfortable option of calling for a cab with an Uber app. The same is happening with supermarkets that started to sell online. They have overcome good location and well-known famous supermarkets because they bring purchases right to the door. We have to keep in mind that there is no possibility of predicting the market it is a living organism that reacts to an almost infinite number of factors.

More than that, we are facing the 4th industrial revolution that comes with a much broader vision of industries, where processes are managed by a variety of innovative methods, including artificial intelligence. A fully automated scale of industries is not the future. Today, there are many enterprises where people are just checking systems and improving them instead of working with production and the product itself. In other words, people work more and more with technology and development of systems. Hence, those who are learning today in schools will hardly ever work on manual productions because they are already uncompetitive. Almost all industrial productions in all sectors are already on the way to reorganization into the new industry standard. Robotics and artificial intelligence do many functions where humans are not sufficient. That dramatically changes the structure of industries and economics. This approach enables increasing the capacity of production in almost any industrial sector unbelievably quickly if needed. The only real limitation usually is the demand on the market, that is mostly connected with consumer preferences, promotion and price level. Development of a product that matches the consumer's quality and price expectations can trigger an increasing demand in the short term. However, the development of a known brand name usually takes years. Therefore, Ukraine can accelerate reform of old industrial infrastructure by cross-border investments into production on Ukrainian territory that will produce for non-Ukrainian brand names at the beginning. This approach has quickly developed economies of far East countries and can be successfully used in Ukraine as well. It is worth mentioning that it is a suitable moment for this approach, production prices in China are increasing because of the growing standard of living and internal consumption. Cross-border investments would create sustainable workplaces and understanding of innovative approaches for the further development of the industrial sector. Nonetheless, such investments will not come without qualified and active specialists ready to implement new technologies. Educational level is critical in the era of modern technologies.

EDUCATION

The Ukrainian educational system still cannot prepare modern professional specialists and this is the most significant problem where many other troubles are rooted. Although Ukraine has one of the best higher education enrolment rates in the world[22], the current higher education system in Ukraine is mostly a legacy of the Soviet era. Centralized, stagnant and isolated Soviet education was built on hopeless backwardness. After the collapse of the Soviet Union, bureaucratic structures exaggerated further, with extremely low salaries for teachers and post-Soviet understanding (still dominating in Ukraine), that education is not about increasing qualification, but a formal routine for getting a diploma. Another myth is that one can get a job, not because of technical skills or professional knowledge, but only thanks to connections and personal relations. Therefore, there is no data about the employment of graduates. Universities are not interested in this information. Links between universities and business are still in their infancy in Ukraine today, with almost no history of creating them. Most employers have little ability to exert influence on universities and there have been almost no initiatives to link university study with jobs.[23] There is neither support nor help for students to find jobs. For many, parental connections or the black market are the realities of job finding.[24] This situation demonstrates how universities pre-program the new generation to become members of a corrupt society. Universities in Ukraine are still suffering from

---

[22] According to Ministry of Education and Science Newsletter (August 2015) Ukraine ended up with 70% of 18-year olds enrolling in higher education. That was 1.7 m. students in a country of 45 m. people.
[23] British Council 2015, 7.
[24] British Council 2015, 8.

international isolation, deep corruption, and incredibly inefficient use of funds. Ukraine needs modern, European and not marginal post-Soviet universities.

After the Revolution of Dignity, revolutionary reforms have also started in the educational sector. Massive cuts of teaching posts drastically reduced the number of higher education institutions[25]. Introducing new legislation to combat the educational problems in Ukraine by dismantling the system of central ministry control, and replacing it with financial, academic and administrative autonomy for universities,[26] has fostered the development of a new breed of higher education institutions. The primary target is to transform the concept of higher education centered on diploma into centers of innovation and independent thought. Instead of creating clerks and employees submissive to old bureaucratic systems, universities should train inspired, creative and open-minded people that can quickly adapt to changes in the world. They should be self-sufficient, able to create new working places and earn a living by themselves, instead of depending on the system, expecting it to take care of them. Universities should be transformed into strong centers, where creators of the future of the country are educated. Students should become active and responsible citizens able to take care of their country. They should create and promote initiatives that are connected with the needs of the people; those initiatives should be able to compete with corporate and political interests of lobbyists. This would make universities genuine centers of thought, a concentration of potential of the country, places where a new generation learns how to create the wealth of the society they live in. At the moment this potential in Ukraine is still mobilized on behalf of oligopolies which, instead of creating the wealth of the society, shamelessly rob it. Today, asymmetry of information, incredible contrasts of poverty and riches, the inability to solve problems of society and other negative issues of Ukraine are mainly rooted in the lack of skills and education of the society. The most successful EU countries like Denmark, Sweden, Germany and others

---

[25] From over 800 with a target to have 100.
[26] Tatsenko 2014.

educate new generations with a strong accent on creativity and the entrepreneurial spirit. How do they do that?

STARTUPS

Students have the best opportunity to start developments in different spheres during their studies in universities. They can learn technology by practicing and participating in development. Universities in Ukraine are establishing workshops and centers of development where active students start to develop their startups and, what is most important, they enter the worldwide market. Universities create a place for startups where students get their first contracts even during their studies. As self-driven citizens that are not using but creating employment; they start to create not only their future but also the wealth and prosperity of the country. Universities are centers of a creative atmosphere, which motivate and encourage the next generation to be able to build the country of tomorrow. Almost 20,000 European startups in various workshops are expected in 2018. They will challenge to disrupt industries in the harsh reality of the marketplace that is extremely crowded already. However, what are those workshops for? Experts have noticed that experienced industry enterprises have very well-organized processes for development of new technologies, services, or products from a concept through many tests and prototyping to final implementation. This same approach is professionally maintained and groomed in workshops for startups. More than that, there is no need to invest in resources and assets for each startup separately because the coefficient of the success of a startup is usually less than 10%. Investment in a workshop can cover many startups. Some workshops in Europe operate thousands of startups each year. Those investments have very high value-return because they are not only small but also because many ideas and trials can be tried on one platform: in other words, those investments are reversible. However, investment into one corporate business, in case of a wrong strategy, is irreversible and will bring losses. Workshops are usually equipped with new digital technologies, prototyping machinery, software frameworks and studios that make creation, prototyping, testing and promoting new products unbelievably fast.

There is no need for redundant bureaucratic schemes and significant investments into each startup separately because many startups can use the same workshop for everybody. There is a vast gap in post-Soviet countries between those who are initiative, active and able to risk and those who are not. However, success stories of startups change the mentality of society dramatically because the attention of the population is focused on positive and fruitful ideas shaping the future of the country. It seems that Ukrainians have already understood that. Workshop culture has started in Ukraine and has already reached a high level with startup centers in Kyiv, Lviv, and Kharkiv. They are promising. Those workshops already receive some funds. Lack of funds for startups and deliberate creation of new modern workplaces in Ukraine can turn into a wave of emigration to other European countries to find better- paid jobs. Access to global markets and jobs outside the country is an essential option for the low-income population that cannot find jobs locally, especially for those who cannot feed themselves or their families. Emigration will grow significantly in any case, but without creating a culture of startups and support for newly born entrepreneurs in Ukraine, it may be devastating. What can we expect from the trend of startups, how will it transform Ukraine's situation where wealth is still disproportionately concentrated in oligopolies?

REFORMS

Wealth in Ukraine is still concentrated in the hands of a few owners of oligopolies. But no enterprise can operate without healthy and qualified workers. Therefore, those same oligopolies inevitably depend on human resources. It is worth mentioning that the workers are those same citizens who decided not to suffer from poverty and crime anymore, those who have enough character to make a choice and fight for their dignity. Workers can demand attention to their requests. They can stop the work of the enterprise if an owner is too busy to meet with them and take requests of workers seriously. They have already learned how to create communities and are learning how to create employment. Also, they are discovering increasingly wider possibilities to emigrate to other European countries to find better-paying jobs. In fact, they are already doing all of this, but the extent is still small in comparison with what it would be if so-called oligarchs will not take note of the changing situation. Workers are starting to address the issue of a safe environment for living and working. They already have all of the options to remove obstacles which block the potential of the society and growth of wealth of the country. Engaging with the culture of unions and communities, which are concerned to solve their problems with support from the government and participation of corporations, is the most efficient accelerator for growth of the wealth of the country. Creation of effective communities can generate constantly renewed improvement and programs for problem solution. This can lead to significant stabilization of the environment, regarding safety, prevention of corruption, reduction of crime – even if the wealth of society would rise slowly. Instead of concentrating the wealth disproportionately, it would be equalized the wealth among communities, among those who are actively solving their everyday problems. In other words, to stabilize the situation and establish the safety in the country, there is an unavoidable need for active and responsible people who are supporting each other through community relations and activities. But what should we start from, what can be done to overcome this difficult period with minimum losses?

Ukraine's economy depends heavily on Soviet heritage factories built as vertical type organizations that are incredibly inefficient, not competitive in the global market, risky and extremely expensive to maintain and transform. Internal structures are thoroughly corrupt and muddled with personal relations, which are almost impossible to transform without entirely changing the personnel. Often it is more optimal to build a new technological structure with new codes and regulations from scratch, instead of taking old infrastructure with old codes and regulations and transforming it. Also, it is important to note that instead of preserving isolated corporate monoliths, a more optimal way is a creation of open modules that will facilitate safer and more sustainable industrial environments in Ukraine. This approach is like the creation of Lego parts that empower the emergence of almost unlimited possibilities for growth, of large industrial formations, instead of a few centralized isolated oligopolies that can look simpler for the short term but can quickly become obsolete and extremely hard to reform in case of changes in market preferences. The very vertical integration is backward since many modern corporations[27] have no production lines. They are engaged in development and marketing, not in production itself. It is too risky to depend on a set of production limitations because technologies are changing very fast. It is easier to change the supplier than abandon one's production when a technology becomes obsolete. Even in very conservative markets, like the automotive industry, where safety and quality are especially critical, each car today has elements from thousands of suppliers[28]. Instead of concentrating everything on one modern production, corporations have become well organized modular structures of suppliers, investing in innovative development teams and marketers of the brand.

There are also strong tendencies of modular structures inside industrial enterprises. Departments are transformed into self-driven modules that can be easily transformed or sold if needed. Smaller teams of entrepreneurs are flexible and have high irreversibility of investment because investments can be reused in a changing situation. Even in case of a failure, small teams can quickly readapt and restart to face new challenges of the market with new approaches using comparatively small resources. There are more chances to succeed in this way; therefore, establishing smaller and flexible self-driven parts of big enterprises, in the long term can comprise much more optimal investments. This tendency is evident in all sectors, the most visible of them being software corporations[29], where changes require complex and rapid predictions and are very prognostic about the rest of the market. Very few people in flat organizations compose a hierarchy. Instead, they follow a small-company-family model. Fast-growing organizations follow a so-called flat structure, organized into self-driven

---

[27] Apple, Adidas, Nike, etc.
[28] Audi has over 1200, Tesla over 2000 different suppliers in each model.
[29] Google, Wix, etc.

companies and guilds. The trend of flat organizations, composed of comparatively small-sized, self-driven modules, is a growing organizational tendency of the world's largest companies. This naturally brings openness, innovativeness, "hands-on the pulse," and the possibility of rapid growth. Everybody is responsible for his area and can take quick decisions. Also, it leaves a space for equal human relations because everybody is virtually on the same level. One of the most critical aspects of such an approach for us is that it follows the already mentioned trend of dignity and concentration on individual's self-worth. Even new products in corporations often start as new startups that grow later to worldwide recognition.

CLUSTERS

Small and medium-sized startups could grow even faster than in universities if they had access to professional resources of technical potential and could source know-how from experienced enterprises. If ineffective Ukrainian enterprises, especially those that belong to the state and are unsurmountable burden for the country or profit-losing factories surviving on subsidiaries, would support the creation of workshops, startup formations would begin to appear by their side. Those big enterprises would benefit from smaller, dynamic self-driven startups that do not cost the enterprise but can develop innovative technical solutions, provide quality services or create marketable products. Smaller-sized startups can be quickly restructured, sold or closed if no longer needed without an impact on the main enterprise. Each startup team can decide how many employees it needs, how to organize itself to be profitable, where to source, and what product or service to concentrate on. Through the help of larger enterprises, there would be no need to invest in assets of startups entering the industrial sector. Workshops and shared resources would empower different startups with opportunities, equipment or services on a rental basis. Also, the growth of a certain number of such startups would enable profitability of such workshops and further expansion of systems of sharable resources. At the moment a lot of large factories in Ukraine are on the edge of bankruptcy. Only in 2017, the implementation of the economic policy of the government resulted in a decrease in the number of economically active enterprises by 4%.

Without changing the economic policy Ukraine is on the verge of becoming a cemetery of dead factories with tremendous losses of industrial capacity. Any business in difficult situations tries to sell or close non-profitable parts or units and start to outsource those services or products from other suppliers if needed. Still, in Ukraine in the event inefficient allocation of resources the government subsidizes or refinances those enterprises to save jobs in a region and guarantee economic stability. Many large enterprises in Ukraine survive because of subsidies and support mechanisms initiated by the government of the country. At the same time, it is a good opportunity for the government. Those non-profitable units, for instance, laboratories, logistics or marketing departments, could be evaluated from the perspective of working not only for one corporation but for the global market if they could be restructured into self-driven and profitable enterprises with professional consultants from universities, for example. The maximum value could be created if that program would be united and integrated with academic potential by tenders to universities. The university that prepares the best scenario and strategy of the unit, technology or product would win the tender. Graduate after graduate would become better and better preparing the plans for preservation and growth of the economy of the country. If universities could get necessary funds for startups in such a way, those funds would be dramatically smaller and far more efficiently used than those that usually are invested into large enterprises and dissolve due to corruption schemes with very little, if any, lasting positive effect.

Development or supporting of large enterprises, their departments, their products or their services would be reliable and safe, provided they would develop as the self-driven, profitable modular units able to survive independently from the large enterprise. Before their bankruptcy, not efficient, large enterprises could be transformed into smaller manageable divisions. Those divisions could operate as separate and self-driven profitable businesses, sourcing needed services and materials from each other naturally fighting for profitability, best price and quality issues. They can actively search for new possibilities and new worldwide markets for their products or services. This could save a lot for the country in case of bankruptcy of oligopolies in fierce competition. There is no one rule for various situations because each enterprise is different, but it is clear that each division should become modular and profitable. This strategy could preserve from loss valuable resources of large enterprises that at the moment are processing as monoliths and could create an ecosystem of strong clusters. Instead of stagnation of isolated monolithic industries, this approach would shift development of clusters with a concentration of interconnected businesses, suppliers, and associated institutions in a particular field. Parallel development of independent private structures would compete and complement each other. Thus, even in strategic sectors, like a building of new roads or security services, there is no necessity for the domination or strict control by the state. Governmental support and regulations are supposedly needed only to adjust taxes or other regulations to monitor excessive deviations from socially optimal balance, deviations that disrupt democratic and liberal relations. Although there can be no one rule for all situations, those regulations should always follow the highest public benefit.

PUBLIC VALUE

Therefore, the market is not a source of good or evil but a powerful economic engine that must be accorded sufficient space to do its work while also appropriately guarded[30] because any business needs a community, and any community needs the business. No business can operate without workers, and no community can survive today without salaries that in one way or another are generated by businesses. Businesses generate taxes and wealth creation opportunities for citizens of the country.

---

[30] Etzioni 2000, 12.

Communities provide public assets and a supportive environment.[31] If those connections are not appreciated, both sides suffer. People leave for a better place with better opportunities, to another city or emigrate to another country. The region without people loses potential that it had before. That happened on a large scale in Poland and Lithuania. Restoration of lost human resources is incredibly slow. The same applies to the business, without the necessary resources it shrinks or goes bankrupt, creating cascades of losses for owners, partners, employees and the whole country. Rebuilding business infrastructure takes much time. Ukraine already saw neoliberal economic programs which were directed from the top and empowered the growth of corrupt systems at the expense of society. Such strategies are a synonym for the destruction of both the economy and society. Therefore, another method should be considered, not from the top of political sphere and oligopolies, but from the grassroots of society, developing sustainable communities and positive social environments. This direction creates not the personal, but *shared value*.

A growing number of companies[32] have already embarked on significant efforts to create *shared value* by reconceiving the intersection between society and corporate performance.[33] The shared value concept is dedicated to establishing a healthy interrelationship between business and society. The shared value strategy is inseparable from its social impact and understanding that major business opportunities lie in integrating business and society. This means that corporate benefit should be evaluated not just as chasing for profit per se, but also from the standpoint of society. The growth of economy can be reached via egalitarian shared value strategy when investments follow the lines of shared value and creating returns to society. This happens naturally when social factors are viewed in the same picture with economic and competitive results of an enterprise. A prosperous society can be created by realizing that there are social issues that matter. The company should not look like it is evil or harmful to the world people live in. The economic success of the enterprise and future of

---

[31] Porter & Kramer 2011, 56.
[32] Such as GE, Google, IBM, Intel, Johnson & Johnson, Nestlé, Unilever, and Wal-Mart, Tesla, etc.
[33] Porter & Kramer 2011, 56.

the company can be reached by the creation of a product that makes enterprise innovative along with a shared value horizon. In other words, borders between society and business should be dismantled. The success of a company and the success of the community can become mutually reinforcing. Typically, the more closely tied a social issue is to the company's business, the higher the opportunity to leverage the firm's resources, capabilities, and benefit to society.[34] That is why in successful modern companies shared value practices and responsible investments become hard to distinguish from the day-to-day business of the company. Modern companies naturally create shared value because technical improvements naturally push out old ineffective approaches and bring environmentally safe and community-friendly solutions.

We should not be mistaken that talk about the economy, markets and products become significant only when these are connected with heavy industries. Remember that not so long ago, the largest retailer in the world was selling used books.[35] Another group of famous entrepreneurs started from finding text content on web pages.[36] The largest taxi service provider in the world is worth more than half of Ukraine's GDP and started less than ten years ago when two guys were not able to get a cab late night in winter.[37] Moreover, it is not about corrupt relations with governments or private connections to resources. Their growth to the most prominent entrepreneurs in the world started without any protectionism or fraud schemes. Virtually anybody can do this. There is an inconceivably vast market for almost any small thing in the world. Self-driven prosperous society can be created via motivating people to create and sell their products instead of selling themselves. Selling themselves for new generations becomes a synonym of losing dignity. Selling products, not only in a narrow consumer sense but also created things of art, science and the like, encourage the growth of educated, creative and active, self-driven, wealthy society. Therefore, motivation and nurture of self-driven society create the most significant public value. There are ample possibilities to

---

[34] Porter & Kramer 2006, 2.
[35] Amazon.
[36] Google.
[37] Uber.

become self-driven for almost all professions: scientists write books and get honorariums, doctors have their private offices, that people prefer more than the state healthcare system. The same is valid even for pedagogues, who give private lectures or sell their teaching courses online, or linguists who create grammar checking systems. Some of them start their schools of music or ballet, for instance. No borders between people the possibilities to express themselves and to earn a living can be left out. All spheres that have been blocked from the population by oligopolies and even those which were monopolized by the state should become available except, of course, some public safety organizations.

CONCLUSION

The discussed ideas, approaches and solutions should not be taken as the only possible or finalized concepts, but rather as considerations for further discussions. This overview is an attempt to explicate the insights guiding to the nurturing of the self-driven society. Although there are positive examples to learn from, there are no predefined schemes, because every society is a living and naturally changing organism, which should be respected and supported. There are still many obstacles in Ukraine. Nonetheless, there is also hope that educational reforms and anti-corruption activities are not the formal bureaucratic ceremonies. Those initiatives are coming from the understanding of many Ukrainians that future of their country is related to a sustainable and dignified society. Therefore, a target of the new government is not only to reposition chairs of the nomenclature but to support free-standing, self-driven active citizens. Hence, the focus should be moved from bureaucratic systems, politics, and oligarchs to the people of the country and their needs. People should care about people.

Ukraine could be recreated from new generations that are coming with waves of new graduates every year. Thousands of students graduate this year, but only a few of them are prepared for the changes in their country. However, the potential of education has not been used. It should be unlocked. Students should be taught how to apply their capabilities for the benefit of themselves and the country instead of leaving them trapped inside bureaucratic and corrupt systems. Investments in research and innovation via universities would encourage the new spirit of development and education. Such an atmosphere would develop the new economy and politics of the country based on the science. That, in turn, would raise the reputation of education as new centers of power of the country. Together with the establishment of workshops and involvement of students in startups and forums from the very beginning of their studies, would create the fundaments for the middle class and raise the standard of living. In this way, people grow, not only in qualification but also personally, becoming self-driven, responsible for what they do, and for the environment they live in.

Entrepreneurship is an excellent vehicle for creating jobs and wealth. There is a way to use it by meeting human needs and putting aside the narrow conception of capitalism that has prevented business from providing its potential to meet society's broader challenges. However, the business environment in Ukraine, which is still centered on inefficient schemes, should be transformed and prepared for investments. The concentration of ownership of resources of the country in the hands of few is very ineffective and risky today. The ownership should be distributed amongst new type leaders, those who are open, active, responsible, purpose-oriented, and have the necessary qualifications. There is a growing understanding in Ukraine that this can be done via education. It is worth noting, that encouragement of new generation people is critical because people feel enabled and empowered when their opinions, initiatives, and decisions matter. Such people can remove any impediments. They can change the environment of the country. In other words, those who dominate today, who are addicted to corruption can be replaced by the people educated with a different mentality.

We can summarize, that there is hope that although the situation is still very problematic, the reforms are so vast and unprecedentedly revolutionary that the growth of the country in coming years would not be unexpected. That will be the natural outcome of the innovative and advanced processes in society, economy, and politics of the country. It seems that Ukrainians understand what they are doing and that they chose a liberal democratic direction, not by chance. Political actions here revealed that people of this country are mature enough and have the character to change not only the course of historical geopolitical events but also their corrupt neoliberal model to socially oriented liberal democracy. It is just the start, but it already shows that Ukrainians can nurture a creative, active and self-driven generation via education. It is worth mentioning that undeveloped countries can develop rapidly because of a critical need to replace old corrupt, ineffective schemes. Ukraine can transform and rise much faster than one can expect, it has good foundations to participate in international collaboration projects, both on a small and large scale. There are all necessary conditions and support for fundamental and positive transformations in Ukraine. That can be done via growth of self-driven society and for the benefit of it.

REFERENCES

British Council. 2015. *Higher Education in Ukraine: Briefing Paper.* December 2015.

Chomsky, Noam. 2017. *Neo-Liberalism: An Accounting.* https://youtu.be/U7EyfO0TRm4?t=2890.

Crotty & Kang-Kook, James Crotty and Kang-Kook Lee. 2002. *A Political-Economic Analysis of the Failure of Neoliberal Restructuring in Post-Crisis Korea.* University of Massachusetts, Amherst

Etzioni, Amitai. 2000. *The Third Way to a Good Society. Demos.* Printed in Great Britain by Redwood Books.

Fukuyama, Francis. 2017. *Francis Fukuyama in conversation with Andriy Shevchenko on political disruption.* https://www.youtube.com/watch?v=l46Xvpcsl_k.

Guriev & Rachinsky, Sergei Guriev and Andrei Rachinsky. 2005. The Role of Oligarchs in Russian Capitalism. *Journal of Economic Perspectives.* Volume 19, Number 1. Winter 2005. pp 131–150.

Huntington P. Samuel. 1996. *The Clash of Civilizations and the Remaking of World Order*. New York: Simon & Schuster.

James, Crotty. 2000. *Slow Growth, Destructive Competition, and Low Road Labor Relations: A Keynes-Marx-Schumpeter Analysis of Neoliberal Globalization.*

Kotz M. David. Russia's Financial Crisis: The Failure of Neoliberalism? *Z Magazine*, January, 1999, 28-32. Economics Department Thompson Hall, University of Massachusetts Amherst, U.S.A.

Mason J. W. 2016. *James Crotty and the Responsibilities of the Heterodox.* https:// www.ineteconomics.org/ perspectives/ blog/ james-crotty-and-the-responsibilities-of-the-heterodox.

Porter & Kramer, Michael E. Porter and Mark R. Kramer 2006. *Strategy & Society: The Link between Competitive Advantage and Corporate Social Responsibility*. Harvard Business Review.

Porter & Kramer, Michael E. Porter and Mark R. Kramer 2011. *The Big Idea: Creating Shared Value*. Harvard Business Review.

Rybak, Vitalii. 2017. *10 Things You Should Know About Ukraine's Pension Reform.* http://ukraineworld.org/2017/10/10-things-you-should-know-about-ukraines-pension-reform/.

Stedman Jones, Daniel (2012). *Masters of the Universe: Hayek, Friedman, and the Birth of Neoliberal Politics*. Princeton University Press. ISBN 0691151571.

Tatsenko, Lyudmila. 2014. Why Ukraine is reforming its higher education system. *British Council*, 19 June 2014.

Ukraineworld. 2017. *Novopskov Local Community Prospers Due to Decentralisation.* http://ukraineworld.org/2017/10/novopskov-local-community-prospers-due-to-decentralisation/.

INDEX

#

4th industrial revolution, 84

A

abolition, 6, 9, 16, 23, 74
academic experiences, 34
access, 25, 38, 42, 44, 52, 61, 67, 77, 91
accountability, 73, 75
adjustment, 39, 43
administrators, viii, 7, 34, 35, 38, 48
age, 3, 8, 15, 51
aid- dependent, 39
alienation, 21, 67
ambiguity, 57
ambivalence, 56, 57, 62
assessment, 49, 56, 65
assets, 87, 91, 94
asymmetry of information, 86
atmosphere, 54, 87, 97
attitudes, 40, 44, 58
austerity measures, 43
authorities, 45, 52, 73, 80
autonomy, 6, 16, 38, 61, 86
awareness, 15, 16, 22, 35, 60, 63, 67

B

backwardness, 71, 85
bankruptcy, 82, 83, 92
barriers, 74, 83
base, 38, 53, 56, 57, 61
benefits, 10, 37, 57, 59, 60, 75
bullying, 52, 66
bureaucracy, 76, 77
businesses, 12, 93

C

capitalism, 7, 28, 36, 45, 52, 58, 66, 97, 98
career development, 60, 63
challenges, viii, 21, 34, 37, 43, 44, 49, 52, 57, 62, 67, 90, 97
cities, 72, 82
citizens, 2, 11, 25, 71, 73, 74, 76, 78, 79, 80, 86, 87, 88, 93, 96
civilization, 14, 15, 16, 24, 27
clusters, 91, 93
collegiality, 51
commercialization, 46

commodification, 46, 66
common sense, 35, 38
communities, vii, ix, 12, 24, 25, 27, 48, 52, 54, 58, 69, 71, 72, 74, 79, 80, 89, 93, 94, 95, 99
competition, viii, 5, 34, 37, 55, 56, 57, 58, 75, 82, 93
competition and individuality, 55
competitive environment, 37, 55
complexity, 18, 19, 21
computer, 21, 24
conception, 4, 5, 7, 19, 97
consciousness, 10, 12, 21, 26
consumers, 26, 80, 83
consumption, 7, 36, 84
contract of lecturers, 50
contradictions and uncertainties, 57
controversial, 17, 37
convenience sampling, 41
correlation, 20, 73
corruption, ix, 17, 70, 71, 82, 86, 89, 92, 96, 97
cost, 43, 44, 46, 75, 91
cost sharing, 43
creativity, 27, 80, 81, 83, 87
cross-border investments, 84
culture, 9, 15, 17, 21, 22, 25, 45, 88, 89
curriculum, viii, 34, 38, 43, 45, 46, 48, 62, 64, 65
curriculum development, 46, 62

D

danger, 3, 78
debt relief, 40
dedication, 4, 9, 40, 58
democracy, vii, ix, 2, 8, 10, 13, 16, 17, 36, 38, 65, 69, 70, 73, 74, 98
deregulation, 39
destiny, 2, 4
destruction, 21, 94

developing countries, 38, 74
dignity, 70, 71, 72, 76, 77, 83, 88, 91, 95
discomfort, 42, 57
distribution, 64, 80
doctors, 9, 96
dominance, 12, 37

E

economic efficiency, 50, 58
economic growth, 7, 37, 38
economic outcomes, 46
economic policy, 76, 92
economics, 38, 80, 84
ecosystem, vii, ix, 69, 93
education, vii, viii, 2, 7, 8, 9, 11, 13, 14, 15, 16, 17, 21, 22, 24, 27, 33, 34, 35, 37, 38, 40, 43, 50, 60, 63, 64, 65, 66, 67, 71, 77, 80, 85, 86, 96, 97, 98, 99
educational institutions, vii, ix, 34, 35, 60, 62
educational reforms, 43, 44, 45, 96
educational system, 35, 85
effective communities, 89
election, 38, 39
employees, 50, 81, 86, 91, 94
employment, ix, 48, 70, 77, 80, 85, 87, 89
employment opportunities, 48
entrepreneurs, 88, 90, 95
entrepreneurship, viii, 34
environment, 20, 37, 55, 56, 70, 75, 78, 80, 83, 89, 94, 97
equality, v, vii, 1, 2, 3, 5, 7, 8, 9, 10, 11, 13, 14, 16, 17, 23, 25, 26, 27, 77
equipment, 76, 91
ethical issues, 42
ethics, 17, 37
evolution, 70, 73
exclusion, 3, 22, 50
expertise, 24, 27
exploitation, 39, 80

explorative research, 41
exports, 26, 39

F

factories, 89, 91, 92
fear, 4, 45, 54, 55, 76
feasibility, 41
feelings, 40, 72
financial, 43, 44, 48, 61, 74, 75, 76, 78, 86
financial institutions, 75, 78
fiscal policies, 40
formation, 9, 44
foundations, 77, 98
freedom, v, vii, 1, 2, 3, 5, 7, 8, 9, 10, 11, 13, 14, 15, 16, 17, 23, 25, 27, 56
funding, 7, 38, 45, 46, 48, 56, 61
funds, 48, 79, 81, 86, 88, 92

G

Ghana Poverty Reduction Strategy (GPRS 1) policy, 40
global economy, 13, 83
global markets, 82, 88
globalization, vii, 2, 14, 24, 28, 29, 74, 75, 82, 99
governance, 2, 35, 36, 38, 39, 51
government subventions, 43
governments, 17, 95
grading systems, 47
grassroots, 72, 94
growth, 7, 73, 74, 75, 81, 89, 90, 91, 92, 94, 95, 97

H

hair, 12, 26
health, 7, 9, 10, 17, 20, 22, 27, 58

higher education, v, vii, viii, 15, 33, 34, 35, 38, 40, 42, 43, 50, 60, 62, 64, 65, 66, 67, 85, 86, 98, 99
HIPC initiative, 40
history, 18, 19, 22, 67, 85
horizon, 2, 19, 20, 22, 95
human, ix, 4, 5, 9, 13, 15, 18, 28, 36, 46, 69, 70, 71, 73, 78, 81, 83, 88, 91, 94, 97
human activity, 5, 81
human dignity, 70, 78
human resources, 88, 94
human right, 9, 13

I

identity, 3, 14, 21, 24, 27, 38, 63, 72
ideology, viii, 20, 26, 33, 34, 36, 38, 45
imagery, 15, 26
images, 15, 17, 21, 26
independence, 5, 43, 72, 80
individualism, ix, 34, 55, 56, 62
individuals, 21, 25, 35, 37, 41, 44, 47, 51, 52, 56, 62, 70, 79
industries, 44, 81, 84, 87, 90, 93, 95
inequality, 3, 5, 6, 12, 67, 74, 77
infrastructure, 59, 71, 81, 84, 89, 94
instability and risk, 55
institutions, viii, 5, 8, 14, 15, 16, 33, 35, 37, 38, 41, 42, 43, 44, 45, 47, 48, 49, 50, 52, 58, 59, 60, 62, 63, 75, 86, 93
institutions of higher education, 37
investment, 75, 76, 83, 87, 90
investments, 7, 75, 78, 81, 83, 84, 87, 88, 90, 94, 97
issues, 4, 14, 42, 59, 79, 86, 93, 94

L

landscape, 50, 60
laws, 3, 5, 6, 16, 17, 23
leadership, 12, 66, 67

learning, 42, 43, 44, 47, 54, 58, 61, 66, 84, 89
learning and curriculum, 43
learning outcomes, 42, 54, 58
liberal democracy, ix, 10, 69, 73, 74, 98
liberalism, vii, 2, 3, 4, 8, 9, 10, 11, 12, 14, 16, 17, 23, 24, 25, 26, 27
limited resources, 52, 62
limited shared governance, 51
living conditions, 24, 27, 79
local communities, 78, 79, 80
logistics, 80, 92

M

machinery, 11, 87
majority, 7, 44, 48, 56, 62, 74
management, ix, 10, 18, 34, 38, 43, 50, 51, 54, 58, 61, 80
manufacturing, 70, 82
marketing, 81, 90, 92
marketization, 46, 50, 66
marketplace, 87
mass, 26, 79
matter, 23, 26, 51, 94, 97
media, 25, 65, 71, 83
mental health, 57, 59
mentoring, 35, 53, 60, 64, 66, 67
meritocracy, ix, 34, 62
methodology, 35, 40, 43
Middle East, 14, 15, 16, 22, 23, 25
military, 8, 13, 14, 16, 39
mission, 42, 76
mission reports, 42
models, 7, 51, 81
modern economies, ix, 69
modernization, 22, 72
modules, 89, 90
motivation, 59, 95
murder, 12, 15, 77

N

national dignity, 72, 77
national identity, 72, 83
nationalism, 12, 25, 71, 72
nationalists, 15, 22, 23
negative emotions, 58, 62
neglect, 9, 76
neoliberal ideologies, viii, 34, 35, 38, 40, 41, 43, 44, 45, 50, 59, 60, 63
neoliberalism, v, vii, viii, 28, 33, 34, 35, 36, 37, 39, 40, 41, 42, 44, 45, 50, 56, 57, 59, 60, 62, 63, 64, 65, 66, 67, 69, 70, 74, 75, 76, 80, 99
New Patriotic Party (NPP), 40
North America, 13, 73

O

obstacles, 89, 96
oligopolies, vii, ix, 69, 74, 77, 86, 88, 90, 93, 94, 96
openness, 13, 91
operations, 10, 81
opportunities, ix, 27, 48, 49, 59, 69, 78, 79, 80, 82, 91, 93, 94
organism, 84, 96
ownership, 4, 97

P

participants, 25, 40, 41, 42, 44, 48, 54, 56, 58
personal relations, 85, 89
policy, 36, 40, 41, 43, 47
politics, vii, 2, 10, 12, 39, 65, 67, 72, 73, 74, 75, 76, 78, 80, 82, 96, 97, 98, 99
population, 5, 11, 13, 45, 71, 76, 88, 96
possibility, vii, 2, 4, 18, 19, 20, 21, 22, 73, 84, 91

post-Soviet countries, 80, 88
poverty, 6, 7, 26, 39, 71, 76, 77, 86, 88
primacy, 13, 14
principles, 8, 17, 35, 37, 40, 44, 74, 77
private, vii, viii, 1, 2, 3, 4, 6, 9, 10, 23, 24, 27, 34, 36, 38, 44, 46, 74, 75, 93, 95
private sector, viii, 34, 44
private sources, 46
privatization, 17, 39
profit, 36, 75, 80, 83, 91, 94
profitability, 91, 93
proliferation, 24, 71
promotion, 16, 34, 35, 48, 55, 62, 63, 84
promotion of a sense of belonging, 35, 62
propaganda, 71, 72
prosperity, 37, 73, 76, 87
provision of resources, 35, 61, 63
Provisional National Defense Council (PNDC), 39
public, vii, 1, 2, 3, 4, 5, 7, 8, 9, 10, 12, 14, 16, 23, 33, 36, 37, 38, 40, 41, 47, 65, 66, 67, 76, 93, 94, 95
public affairs, 11, 23
public domain, 2, 3, 5, 6, 9, 10, 14
public universities, 40, 41, 65, 67
public value, 93, 95
publishing, 65, 67

Q

qualifications, 55, 97
qualitative, 40, 64, 65, 67
quality, 26, 34, 43, 44, 47, 57, 66, 79, 84, 90, 91, 93
quality assurance, 34, 47, 66

R

reality, 12, 18, 19, 87
recognition, 10, 14, 21, 71, 72, 73, 91
recommendations, 36

reflexivity, 18, 19, 20, 21
reform, viii, 34, 38, 43, 44, 71, 72, 73, 75, 77, 79, 84, 86, 90, 96, 97, 99
regulations, 89, 93
relevance, 43, 44
relevance of teaching, 43
relief, 6, 40
religion, 12, 18, 23
requirements, viii, 2, 6, 9
resources, 22, 35, 52, 53, 61, 63, 70, 75, 76, 87, 90, 91, 92, 93, 94, 95, 97
response, 41, 49
restructuring, viii, 34, 62
revenue generation, 45
revolution of dignity, ix, 70, 77, 86
rewards, 11, 36
rhetoric, 12, 13
rights, 4, 9, 13, 14, 17, 24, 27
risk, ix, 52, 58, 69, 73, 83, 88
rule of law, 8, 13, 73
rules, vii, 1, 9, 10, 14, 17
Russia, 3, 12, 13, 14, 25, 70, 72, 76, 99

S

safety, ix, 7, 9, 61, 70, 73, 77, 80, 89, 90
school, 15, 41, 84, 96
science, 27, 78, 95, 97
security, 4, 11, 17, 74, 79, 93
segregation, 50, 51, 54, 55, 56, 62
selectivity, 18, 21, 22, 27
self-driven society, ix, 69, 70, 79, 95, 96, 98
self-worth, 62, 91
senior lectureship, 48
sense of ambivalence, 56, 57, 62
services, 24, 27, 46, 81, 87, 91, 92
shared value, 94, 99
signs, 15, 16
skin, 12, 27
SME, 81
social context, viii, 33

social life, 24, 27
social relations, 21, 36
socialist posturing, 39
society, vii, ix, 1, 3, 4, 5, 8, 9, 11, 17, 20, 37, 54, 59, 64, 65, 69, 70, 72, 74, 75, 77, 79, 80, 83, 85, 86, 88, 89, 94, 95, 96, 97, 98
software, 88, 90
solution, 6, 12, 22, 89
Soviet Union, 3, 8, 14, 71, 85
spending, 7, 37, 77
stability, 17, 92
standard of living, 84, 97
startups, 87, 88, 91, 92, 97
state, 3, 7, 11, 12, 16, 19, 23, 34, 36, 37, 39, 40, 73, 77, 91, 93, 96
state intervention, 36, 37
states, 8, 14, 37
strategic, 42, 44, 70, 93
stress, ix, 34, 62, 77
structural adjustment programmes (SAP), 39, 40, 43
structure, 19, 20, 23, 38, 43, 72, 84, 89, 90
student assessment, 49
suppliers, 81, 90, 92, 93
surveillance, 49, 59, 62
survival, 5, 37, 38, 75, 77, 78, 82

T

takeover, 45, 63
target, 47, 73, 83, 86, 96
taxes, 6, 7, 79, 93
teachers, 9, 85
team members, 82, 83
team work, 58
teams, 80, 81, 83, 90
tenure, 44, 56

tertiary education, 41, 44
testing, 81, 88
time reflection, 2
total output and learning outcome, 58
toxic, 56
transformation, ix, 66, 70, 71, 79
transformations, 77, 98
transportation, 24, 27, 82

U

Ukraine, ix, 14, 69, 70, 71, 72, 73, 76, 77, 78, 79, 82, 84, 85, 86, 87, 88, 89, 92, 94, 95, 96, 97, 98, 99
Ukrainian educational system, 85
unhealthy environment, 56
universities, vii, viii, 29, 34, 35, 38, 40, 41, 43, 44, 45, 46, 47, 48, 49, 50, 51, 52, 53, 58, 59, 60, 61, 65, 81, 85, 86, 87, 91, 92, 97
university managers, 41
University Regulatory Council (URC), 43

W

war, 13, 16, 62, 75
wealth, ix, 2, 4, 5, 6, 37, 43, 45, 46, 50, 69, 73, 74, 83, 86, 87, 88, 89, 93, 97
wealth creation, 43, 45, 46, 50, 93
welfare, 36, 39, 79
welfare-state withdrawal, 39
well-being, 10, 80
workers, 7, 9, 37, 48, 52, 64, 80, 88, 93
World Bank, 8, 38, 40, 65, 66
World War I, 8, 14
worldwide, 82, 83, 87, 91, 93
worry, 48, 56

Related Nova Publications

Macroeconomic Policies in Countries of the Global South

Editors: Anis Chowdhury and Vladimir Popov

Series: Economic Issues, Problems and Perspectives

Book Description: The volume examines macroeconomic policies for developing countries. The chapters analyse the kind of macroeconomic policies that are more conducive to inclusive and sustainable growth in developing countries.

Hardcover ISBN: 978-1-53615-752-9
Retail Price: $230

Productive Forces of Design: The Basis of Post-Industrial Development

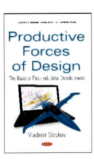

Author: Vladimir Strokov

Series: Economic Issues, Problems and Perspectives

Book Description: A new economy is being considered, in which economic activity of society and a set of relations are taking shape not only at the stages of production, distribution, exchange and consumption, but also at the design stage, forming the basis of post-industrial development.

Softcover ISBN: 978-1-53615-581-5
Retail Price: $95

To see a complete list of Nova publications, please visit our website at www.novapublishers.com

Related Nova Publications

LEGAL FRAMEWORK AND ISSUES IMPACTING THE BUSINESS ENVIRONMENT FACED BY FOREIGN COMPANIES INVESTING IN INDIA: CHALLENGES AND OPPORTUNITIES

AUTHOR: Luciano Pettoello-Mantovani

SERIES: Economic Issues, Problems and Perspectives

BOOK DESCRIPTION: This book deals with the complex and often challenging process for international companies in expanding their business through investing in the Indian emerging market. The process of globalization has allowed for the progressive fading of economic, commercial, and technological boundaries.

SOFTCOVER ISBN: 978-1-53615-091-9
RETAIL PRICE: $95

To see a complete list of Nova publications, please visit our website at www.novapublishers.com